ASSERTIVENESS TRAINING

HOW TO STAND UP FOR YOURSELF, BOOST YOUR CONFIDENCE, AND IMPROVE ASSERTIVE COMMUNICATION SKILLS

CHASE HILL

CONTENTS

YOUR FREE SAY NO CHECKLIST
DON'T LET THE PEOPLE PLEASING TRAP YOU AGAIN...

I'd like to give you a gift as a way of saying thanks for your purchase!

This checklist includes:

- 8 steps to start saying no

- 12 must-dos to stop feeling guilty
- 9 healthy ways to say no

The last thing we want is for your mood to be ruined because you weren't prepared.

To receive your Say No Checklist, visit the link:

www.chasehillbooks.com

Prefer a quick access? Scan the QR code below:

If you have any difficulty downloading the checklist, contact me at **chase@chasehillbooks.com,** and I'll send you a copy as soon as possible.

INTRODUCTION

Sitting through one of my university lectures almost two decades ago, I couldn't figure out why there weren't more subjects in life skills.

Did I really need to know the ins and outs of civil wars? Was this going to help me learn anything about myself? Would memorizing dates to pass an exam teach me to stand up for myself or help me learn to become more confident?

While struggling to memorize factual information, we were never taught vital skills that would allow us to successfully communicate and assert ourselves in the real world.

A degree or qualifications will only take you so far in life. Once you have a job or start a new relationship, it is not easy learning how to communicate in an effective way. This is something I and so many others have struggled with, which is the healthy balance between being too passive and too aggressive.

Being assertive is not a skill we are all born with. When you add this on to a shy personality, it becomes impossible to stand up for ourselves in everyday situations. Gradually, we become more and more worn down until there are significant mental and even physical health problems. We can't continue in a life that is dominated by making other people happy instead of ourselves.

You have spent your life listening to throw around comments like "You need to be more confident" or "Go out and get what you want." Anybody who suffers from a lack of assertiveness knows that this is far from easy.

Our timid personalities lead people to think that we are lacking intelligence, whether practical or emotional. On the contrary, we are smart, hard-working, and highly skillful. Yet it's those that know how to assert themselves that seem to get all the glory.

The other side of the coin is that we worry our assertiveness is going to cause others pain. I feared saying no to people because I worried they would be upset or disappointed. You stop living your life and end up feeling like a vessel for other people to use as they wish, obliged to work overtime, or sit through dreaded family dinners. It is impossible for us to show our true emotions as we are terrified of how others will react. We spend years walking on eggshells.

I spent at least ten years living like this. I was passive, and I was unable to strive for what I really wanted. I constantly said yes to things that would make others happy and didn't have a life of my own. I drifted through life with a fake passion, telling myself that I was a good person.

What hurt the most was when my brother asked his friend to be his best man over me. Unable to express how I really felt, he simply said, "I knew you would be alright with it," and this was the moment I knew I had to make a change. My mind raced back to university and the lack of classes that taught assertiveness, so I became passionate about learning this skill.

This book is a combination of knowledge, exercises, and proven skills for you to start using straight away to see noticeable differences in your life. We are going to work together on understanding some of our most frequent problems surrounding assertiveness.

Experience tells us that it is our lack of confidence, fear of rejection, and guilt that prevent us from being more assertive. However, we won't play the blame game and lay fault on why standing up for ourselves is difficult. Instead, we will look at psychological reasons, but more importantly, focus on the solution.

The need to express how we feel is not limited to just one area of our lives. For this reason, it is important to dedicate time to practical advice for a whole range of situations and relationship dynamics. I am fascinated by behavioral types, and I strongly feel that understanding more about human behavior will also help you to understand the changes that you need to make.

Regardless of whether you consider life to be short or long, it is here to be enjoyed. My hope is that everyone can read this book and start to experience the joy in their lives, be that in your career, your personal relationships, or how you view the world.

We will learn how to set boundaries within our different relationships so that it becomes easier to say no. Everyone deserves the right to express themselves and to be happy, and this is what our goal will be.

Society today seems to be confused about assertiveness and this sends us mixed messages. One minute we should keep our opinions to ourselves so as not to rock the boat, the next we are told that being assertive is necessary to get what we want.

The problem is, finding the balance between being passive and being aggressive is something that we have to learn ourselves, and it's okay to need some help in this area. After all, it can be rather complex.

I have been in your shoes, and I know the change is not easy. This is why I feel it is so important to share my experiences. The day I watched my brother getting married, knowing that I should have been by his side, was the last day of my old life.

I studied, I practiced, and although there were some terrifying experiences, there were also some extraordinary rewards that you too will be able to experience.

Learning is great, but when you are then able to share the knowledge with others, the gratification is tenfold. Which leads me to today. As a life coach, I have been lucky to help hundreds of others to become more assertive without losing their ability to be nice.

I have worked with business people, both men and women, retired people, students, single moms, houschusbands, and everyone in between. Thanks to these people, I have gained more insight into the different situations where being assertive has been necessary. While exploring different personality types, I have been able to put together an effective set of changes that bring forth positive results.

If you are reading this, you have realized that a change is necessary. Let's take the first step by getting a better understanding of assertiveness.

CHAPTER 1: WHAT IS ASSERTIVENESS AND WHY IS IT SO DIFFICULT FOR ME?

L et's start on a positive note. We tend to look at people and see assertiveness as a gift. We envy those who are able to assert themselves and wish we could do the same. Our lack of confidence leads us to feel like it is something that we can't achieve. Assertiveness is a skill, and just like all of the great skills you already possess, you can learn this one.

Assertiveness is the ability to stand up for yourself or other people in a calm, positive way without being aggressive or upsetting others. Assertive people express their thoughts and feelings in an appropriate and respectful manner.

For those who have people pleasing tendencies, who are shy, quiet, or passive, learning how to be assertive is an essential skill that will allow you to communicate with your friends, family, and colleagues in a more productive way. You will no longer need to fear how the other person is going to react because assertiveness is not a bad thing. It's actually a very good skill to have.

People who are assertive can act in their own best interests, and they don't feel guilty or anxious about it. For those who have spent years putting other people's needs and desires before their own, it is a significant change that has to be made, but it is important to remember from here on in that you aren't doing anything that is out of the ordinary.

Let's look at an everyday example of how assertiveness should and shouldn't look.

Sam and Jason are looking to redecorate their living room. Jason wants to paint it a dark blue, but Sam is worried that it would make the whole room look too small. Sam could turn around and say, "That's a stupid idea, and we aren't going to do that!" This would come across as aggressive. She is putting her foot down and not respecting Jason's opinion.

The chances are, Jason is going to feel hurt by this abrupt response, and it might even make him feel angry. You may have had similar experiences when something that should be exciting turns into a full-blown argument.

If Sam had put her assertive skills into play, she would have politely said she wasn't sure about that idea, and perhaps they could go to the store to look at paint samples. This would allow for some inspiration and maybe even an alternative solution.

On the other hand, if Jason had good assertive skills, he too would have been able to diffuse the situation and still get his point across.

It is very true that with the stress we deal with on a day to day basis, it is easy to lose our patience and appear aggressive. Sometimes it is even easier to be passive so as not to rock the boat. Neither of these extremes is good behavior, but they are both easy to correct when you have the right knowledge and tools.

Problems Associated with Not Being Assertive

We aren't going to touch too much on the negatives here. If you are reading this book, then you are probably fully aware of how you are suffering. On the other hand, you could need a little guidance in recognizing that your problems stem from not asserting yourself.

In some cases, the lack of ability to stand up for yourself is because you are very timid and don't feel you have the confidence to speak your mind. If you are a people pleaser, it is often from fear of the consequences for standing up for yourself. One client had a terrible experience saying no to their boss. The boss made a public scene, and this was mortifying for the client, so much so that they had to leave their job. It was a great challenge for this person to regain their confidence so they could start to be more assertive.

People pleasing also leads us to feel guilty for putting our needs or wishes ahead of somebody else. Your friend is busier than you are, so you have to schedule plans when they are free because it would help them out more. Wanting to do something when you are free would just be selfish, right!

When loved ones notice that you are unable to stand up for yourself and say what you actually want to say, it can be hard for them too. A friend at university would always say "I don't mind" any time I asked him what we should do. Neither of us were ever able to make a decision because we were both constantly more concerned about the other person. The irony is that I was blinded by my own lack of assertiveness, and I was hurt that he didn't feel confident to express how he felt.

Partners can get frustrated by the lack of assertiveness. In the beginning, it seems a great thing that they always get what they want, but a successful relationship requires both parties to be equally involved. I have seen relationships fail because one partner was always with their friends. The unassertive person doesn't want to spend so much time with their friends. They feel obliged to do it, and therefore, their other relationships begin to suffer.

Some people can't assert themselves because they feel as if they have a sense of duty or an obligation to others. We are seeing this more and more in today's world with technology at our fingertips. The 9 to 5 concept doesn't exist anymore as we feel like we have to reply to emails and messages as soon as they come in. This is leading to 'Work Stress' which has far more dangerous consequences than we are aware of. Because we are too nice to say no or set our boundaries, we end up being constantly 'on-call,' a slave to our smartphones.

In many situations, when this behavior goes on for too long, we begin to feel overcome with anxiety and even depression. We can get swept into a vicious cycle of unhealthy habits and behaviors. We don't eat properly or sleep well enough, and some people turn to alcohol or drugs. I know how soul-destroying this is, especially when all you want to be is a good person.

Why Is Being Assertive a Good Thing?

Over the years I have found that assertiveness has gained a bit of a bad reputation because people often go too far and come across as aggressive. In reality, being assertive is a healthy form of communication. Here are some of the benefits of asserting yourself and what we are going to work on throughout this book.

Being assertive allows you to:

- Improve your self-confidence and self-esteem
- Gain a better understanding of your feelings
- Be respected
- Enhance your communication skills
- Discover compromise in situations
- Make better decisions
- Experience true, honest relationships
- Lower your stress levels
- Get more satisfaction from your career

One of the first things I had to learn was that being assertive wasn't a bad thing when carried out correctly. Exploring our behavior and how people perceive us can be scary, and it isn't something that is mastered overnight. It is necessary for us to begin by looking at the differences in passive, aggressive, and assertive behaviors so that we can recognize these traits within ourselves.

Understanding the Difference Between Passive, Assertive, and Aggressive

Without sounding like a broken record, as we are never taught these skills, it can feel like we are walking an emotional tightrope. You carefully tread along a thin rope of assertiveness, but a slight imbalance and you'll seem aggressive or passive.

Generally speaking, those who struggle to assert themselves are on the passive side. It is rare that we overstep that mark because our focus is on the feelings of others rather than getting what we want.

What Is Passive Behavior?

Passiveness comes from the need to be liked and that an individual is unable to see themselves as equal to others. Their hopes, desires, and needs are not as important as others. This results in people not expressing how they really feel because they either don't see the value in their thoughts and opinions, or they see their thoughts and opinions as less significant.

It is an unconscious act but being passive means that other people are likely to make decisions for you. You may end up feeling like you aren't in control of your own life.

It may seem like a joke when friends and family try to set you up on dates, but the result is that everybody else is dictating your love life.

When something is asked of a passive person, they have a difficult time saying no despite being too busy. Their response may imply that they have no time, but the other person is unlikely to pick up on this. They only hear that their request has been accepted.

Let's look at how a passive person would answer the question, "Can you cook dinner tonight?"

Their answer might be along the lines of, "Well, I was hoping to order Chinese tonight and watch a film because I am tired, but if I go to the supermarket, I can make a curry dish."

In their hearts, they wanted to finish a long day at work, sit on the sofa, and relax. They have taken into consideration what the other person wants and sees this as more important than what they need.

The passive person will further exhaust themselves to make the other person happy. An assertive response would be, "I can't tonight because I am exhausted. I can do it tomorrow."

One of the principal differences between the two answers is that an assertive person takes the time to analyze whether they are able to cook dinner, and they have responded based on their own needs and considering their other responsibilities.

Being passive runs the risk of people around you learning that you don't say no. Whether this is at work or with your personal relationships, the situation won't just suddenly stop. Instead, you become the go-to person for activities and tasks you don't want to or aren't able to do.

What is Aggressive Behavior?

We might assume aggressive behavior is limited to when people become angry or raise their voice. It can actually involve more acts than this. Interrupting other people when they are speaking, ignoring someone, or just telling someone what to do instead of asking them.

As the receiver of aggressive behavior, you might feel hurt, confused, or frightened. You may question why this person has reacted in this way and assume it is something you have done wrong.

Aggression normally leads to a breakdown in communication because the message is unclear. Anger and frustration could be the only thing that you perceive rather than what the person is actually trying to say.

An aggressive person lacks the ability to praise others for things that have been done well. It is unlikely that you will get a thank you for your efforts. They won't take the time to appreciate the sacrifices you make so that their wishes are fulfilled. It is common for people to misinterpret humor and sarcasm for what it may actually be—another form of aggression.

As we saw with Sam and Jason, Sam's response was aggressive. But, for successful communication, we must look at both sides of the conversation. Jason may have the skills to assert himself. It is also possible that his response is aggressive or passive, leading to further miscommunication.

There will be a more detailed discussion on the passive and aggressive behavior later on in the book, where we take a closer look at how to recognize these types of behaviors and how to find your balance.

Mixed Signals

You may often hear of passive-aggressive behavior, which can also promote confusion and negative feelings. The term passive-aggressive is commonly misused, which is why not everyone is clear on the meaning. On top of this, in terms of culture, it can be rather ambiguous.

Passive-aggressive behavior is loosely defined as inaction when action is expected. Intentionally showing up late to a meeting or event, purposely forgetting things, or not working at your best levels would be examples of passive-aggression. It is a common behavior in the workplace and might come about because the person is struggling to express their emotions.

With regards to people pleasing, we may become passive-aggressive because we want to say no, but we say yes. As it is difficult to use words to talk about how we are feeling, we can develop a negative attitude.

If you ask your boss a question and they don't respond, they are acting in a passive-aggressive manner. This is not fair on you because you are unable to do your job well.

Sarcasm is also a form of passive-aggressive behavior, which leads to the ambiguous part. Sometimes, sarcasm can be humorous, and we would call this a passive-aggressive act. When the sarcasm becomes continuous, it is then known as passive-aggressive behavior.

Some actions that used to be classed as passive-aggressive are now defined as covert aggression, and part of our learning will be on how to deal with such behavior. Covert aggression is the subtle things a person can do to get their own way. People who are covertly aggressive will manipulate and exploit you, which might be from flat out lying, playing the victim, or guilting you into doing something.

Like aggression, it is unlikely that this is a behavior you will often display. That's not to say that those who can't be assertive don't get angry. Our need to say yes to everything is incredibly frustrating, and many times I have become angry with myself and the world. But as a people pleaser, I would never show others this side of me.

Why Is It so Difficult for Me to Assert Myself?

Remember, nobody is to blame here, and each individual may relate to one reason or another. Some people aren't interested in looking deeper at their fear of assertiveness, and they just want to start learning practical skills. I can understand that.

Leaving high school and starting university, you are effectively an adult, but at the same time, you are still easily influenced by what society tells you is right or wrong. We see messages telling us to ask for what we want, but then the next week we are told to go out and take what you want in the world. This creates a mental battle—should I ask, or should I take? Do I assert myself or not?

When asking clients why they felt they weren't able to assert themselves, I got some impressive answers. Many we have already touched on, for example, the guilt of putting yourself first, or the fear that we are going to hurt someone else's feelings. Then there is the fear of not being liked by someone, not getting their approval, or worse, being rejected.

One person felt that she could never get it right. The fear of appearing aggressive was too much, and this kept her in her 'passive bubble.' Any time she tried to stand up for herself, she felt terrible, as if she was only causing herself more suffering. It only takes a couple of bad experiences and the fear of retaliation overcomes us.

I was fascinated by the number of people who didn't want to create a scene and so just went along with the flow. They felt like in certain social situations it would be seen as uncool to make any kind of fuss. Others saw expressing their emotions as a sign of weakness, that today we all need to be strong and there is no room for anxiety or stress.

A lack of assertiveness isn't like a cold or the flu. You don't just wake up one morning and have it. This is a learned behavior that may go as far back as your childhood. It is natural for a child to want to make their parents happy. When they receive approval and love for good behavior, they will continue down this path. So, fear of rejection begins. We do all that we can to make sure those around us are happy and that we aren't punished. This is probably not enough by itself.

It's when other factors combine with this that we start to notice a problem. If you add a very shy personality, you can see how it starts to develop into a more serious issue. Bad experiences expressing yourself can lower your confidence to such a level that you become passive.

You might have had a bad relationship with a dominant partner and, during this time, learned that your opinions don't count and that your needs come last. It can also stem from emotional turmoil or trauma—losing a loved one, divorce, or physical abuse.

That what we fear or makes us anxious isn't going to simply disappear once we put our finger on it. I'm not going to tell you that when you learn to accept your fear of rejection, you will be able to control it. It's a little too simplistic for the complexities of psychology. On the other hand, being aware of why you personally fear being assertive will help you to learn which techniques will assist you.

Before we begin to look at dealing with our negative emotions, I would like you to become an observer. Just spend a day or two watching people in various situations and see how they assert themselves. It could be your parents, your colleagues, people in a restaurant, absolutely anywhere. Try to recognize some of the passive, aggressive, and assertive behaviors we have mentioned in this chapter.

CHAPTER 2: OVERCOMING THE FEAR OF BEING ASSERTIVE

Regardless of the type of thing we would like to improve within ourselves, it is necessary to tap away at the layers of our past and to begin by creating a solid foundation of the future we would like to create for ourselves.

While some people like to get to the roots of their issues (as we mentioned in the previous chapter), others like to begin with a fresh start, a clean canvas to work on. As much as we would love to jump straight into being more assertive, our foundations actually include learning how to deal with our fears and anxieties.

Fear and anxiety are two of the most common feelings that arise when we consider being assertive. Although they are linked in some ways, fear and anxiety are not the same.

Fear is a more specific danger we perceive. Anxiety isn't attached to an object or situation; it is more general. When anxiety comes linked to a specific circumstance, it becomes a fear. Anxiety may arise because of other feelings like mental conflict, shyness, doubt, even boredom. When we experience fear, the fight or flight instinct kicks in.

The idea of speaking in front of a crowd will make many people anxious, but while it is only a thought, there is no imminent danger to cause fear. When you are standing on a stage about to speak to the crowd, fear will overwhelm a person. Some strategies for dealing with fear and anxiety will be the same, for example, deep breathing. This chapter is going to separate how we cope with fear and anxiety when we are learning to become more assertive.

Fears that Arise When Being Assertive

We aren't going to make the wrong assumption that we all fear the same things. Some people might be able to relate to one or several of the fears we are going to discuss. It is also perfectly normal if you have unique fears regarding assertiveness. Some of the more frequent fears related to asserting yourself include:

• There is a strong fear that the other person will become angry, and in some cases, this includes fearing that the other person will become physically violent. This doesn't necessarily mean that you have experienced anger or violence in your past. The person you need to be assertive with may have shown aggressive behavior in the past.

• It is not just the fear of an angry response. The idea that the person in the conversation will not take no for an answer is also scary. We are scared that the other person will not take no for an answer and we will be left having to back down or trying to assert ourselves again.

• You might fear the idea of disappointing the other person. It reminds me of when your parents shouted at you as a kid and you sulked a bit, but nothing hurt more than when they said they were disappointed in you. For some, even the disappointing look is enough to paralyze a person in fear.

• If you have people pleasing traits, the act of not being nice is terrifying. Unintentionally, we still confuse saying no with being mean or that it is going to hurt the other person's feelings. This is something very hard to overcome because being a nice person is a good thing. The fear of being mean means to be replaced with knowing that you can assert yourself and still be nice.

• In social situations, there could be a fear of humiliation and embarrassment. Many times, we don't feel like our beliefs or opinions carry the same weight as everybody else's. The conversation may move to the next election or a new medical study. You have read about the subject, but you fear joining in with the conversation in case others laugh at what you say.

• Fear of rejection is something that all of us need to learn how to cope with at some point in our lives. Normally, this experience is something that we go through during high school. There is a massive need to be accepted in social groups, more so in those early years. Toward the end of these critical years, we start to learn more about ourselves and the friends we want to keep. Not being accepted into certain groups becomes less painful. For people pleasers and the nonassertive, the fear of rejection stays with us as it is linked to the need to be liked.

All of these situations and others are because we are facing danger. We have come to the moment when we need to be assertive. It might be that you are just about to start the conversation and you can feel your legs begin to shake and the color draining from your face.

Why Do We Feel Anxious about Being Assertive?

Our anxious state is due to the contemplation of being assertive. It might start the day before an important conversation or even weeks.

Some people live constantly anxious because of the idea of situations that may require assertiveness. It's not to say this feeling is unwarranted and should be dismissed as something we are making up in our minds. Nevertheless, unlike fear, the situation isn't present.

Being anxious is when you go to a restaurant and worry about having to return your food when you haven't even ordered. There is a possibility that you will have to return the food, but only when you reach that moment does the anxiety become fear.

Essentially, every event or situation that can cause us to feel fear will also cause us to feel anxious.

Psychologists call anxiety a fear-based condition. It is exhausting because it is a constant worry of what might happen, and this is why it can lead to many other health issues.

How to Handle Fear When Being Assertive

When you start to feel the fear building up within you, it is worth concentrating on the following points:

1. Everyone has fears. Fears are one of the basic instincts that we rely on for survival and protection. You could try to logically rationalize it, or you could accept the fact that fears are normal. Rather than focusing efforts to overcome fears, it is more important to learn not to be overcome by them.

2. Use visualization techniques to imagine yourself being assertive without fear. Visualization involves retraining your brain with positive imagery. With great conviction, imagine yourself successfully facing your fears. Take in the sounds and smells you also imagine. By repeating this visual image, you are teaching your brain a new way of thinking.

3. Confront your fear of being assertive as soon as possible. If you know you need to reply to your boss's request, then don't put it off. Otherwise your feelings of anxiety will only increase.

4. Consider the worst-case scenario. It might sound like it contradicts visualizing yourself as assertive; however, if you think about the worst that could happen, it can put things into perspective. If the other person reacts negatively, it is because they lack communication skills. The worst-case scenario for you is that you need to continue working on yours. It's not that your fears are unjustified, just that the extent might not justify the situation.

5. Keep sight of your motivation. If you need to say no to working overtime, imagine what you will be doing instead.

Have you been looking forward to that gym session or the romantic dinner with your partner? Focus on this positive event rather than the fear of the situation.

And the big one:

6. Face your fear. So many clients tell me that this is the hardest part, and I found it helps to understand the science behind this. Studies have shown that exposure to fears gradually alters neuronal activity. Mice were put into a box and received a small shock. The second time they were put in the box, they froze in fear. Over time, and without receiving shocks, the mice became relaxed again once in the box. The same thing happens to us. When we begin to face our fear, it gradually becomes easier.

The trick is to start. When you use the advice in points one to five, you will begin to notice number six taking effect.

Learning to Manage Anxiety

Because anxiety occurs on a more frequent, continuous basis, one of the best ways to learn how to manage it is to make small lifestyle changes. As anxiety can stem from worrying about things that may happen, it is useful to create a strong routine in your life. Knowing what is coming up in your daily schedule helps you to be more prepared and less anxious. Two of the most crucial parts of your routine should be:

1. Regular meals. When we skip meals, our blood sugar levels drop and our body releases cortisol, the stress hormone. A little bit of cortisol is good because you may perform better under

pressure, but if you are an anxious person, you will end up feeling worse.

2. Sleep. Our anxiety increases without sleep. Sleep is a challenge in itself when you are full of anxiety, but it will become easier if you develop a relaxing evening routine. Stay away from caffeine, go to bed at the same time each evening, and exchange the electronic device for a book.

Other methods to effectively cope and even reduce the anxiety you face include:

· **Start doing some exercise** to increase the serotonin and endorphins in your body. The increase in oxygen in your blood will also help you to concentrate more. It doesn't have to be a full-on workout in the gym. It could be a brisk walk in nature, dancing to your favorite songs, or yoga. I am a big fan of Exergames, video games that are exercise because there is such a wide range, and I can fit them into my morning routine, whether it's ten minutes or an hour.

· Greatly **reduce the amount of caffeine** you take in. Caffeine increases the heart rate which can lead to anxiety attacks. Start by reducing your caffeinated drinks and explore others that you might like. Water, green tea, and Valerian root tea are known to reduce anxiety.

· **Understand your triggers.** As with fears, each person's anxiety will be triggered by different things, and more specifically people, when being assertive. I have even noticed that certain smells and songs can trigger anxiety. Try to eliminate the sources of your anxiety when possible. If a colleague makes you feel stressed, steer clear of them unless it is for work-related matters.

· **Change your activity.** Take a moment to breathe when your anxiety starts to rise—don't fight it. After a short moment of accepting your emotions, change your activity. If you have been sitting at your desk, walk away from it for a change of scenery. If you were watching the news, switch to music.

· **Keep your mind active.** If a change of activity wasn't enough, choose an activity that engages the brain. When anxiety begins to rise up, it can start to overthink and add to the negative feelings if your mind isn't engaged in an activity.

Keep your mind active by eating food that stimulates your brain. Draw, even if you are just doodling. Have a small selection of 'brain games' on your phone. Sudoku requires concentration, Prune is a gardening game that lets you cut tree limbs and create a tidy space, and Headspace is a mindfulness and meditation app.

Changing your habits will help to reduce anxiety because the brain is actively participating in other tasks.

Negative Beliefs: Cognitive Distortions

The negative experiences we have had while trying to be assertive remains in our mind and reinforces our bad and negative feelings.

Now, we can learn from all of our bad feelings, but it is necessary that we don't allow these feelings to become stuck with us, and a part of who we are. It's the self-fulfilling prophecy, "I have never been able to assert myself and therefore I never will." The following are things we can do to prevent these thought patterns.

· Identify the thoughts that bring about your anxiety.

· View the situation from different points of view, consider all angles and explanations, remove your emotions, and look at the evidence.

· Talk to yourself the same way you would with your friends. You don't tell your friends that they are going to do badly on an exam, so you shouldn't speak to yourself in the same way.

· Check the rationality of your thoughts with others. This is great for social situations and meeting new people when you want to come across as assertive but are convinced it will go wrong. Talk to friends and family about the experiences they have had in new social settings.

· Re-attribution. Instead of blaming ourselves for everything that has gone wrong, re-attribution involves analyzing situations and seeing who or what else played a role in the past negative experience. It's not the same as blaming others, it is making sure that you are not the only one to take responsibility for things that didn't quite work out.

· The pros and cons of your negative belief. It sounds rather basic but writing a list of the pros of feeling this way and another list of the cons, you will have a visual tool that shows you're the result of your thoughts.

· Be careful of clairvoyant behaviors. I have plenty of clients who would never dream of going to see a fortune teller. Nevertheless, their cognitive distortion leads them to feel they can predict a negative future. The same can be said for reading minds and making assumptions on what a person is thinking based on past experiences.

· Avoid selective abstraction. This is when we remember past experiences but only see the negative things that happened rather than the positive parts. When looking back at your attempts at being assertive, find a positive in each of them. It might be that you practiced a technique that you know doesn't work for you, or you discovered another boundary you are not comfortable with.

Becoming the Master of Your Inner Game

Your inner game can be seen as various different things, but principally, it is the internal battle that you have with yourself, your doubts, and your fears. It's your opinions of yourself, your confidence.

While your inner game can be related to any aspect of your life, romance, career, wealth, etc., it is how we play our inner game with regards to our assertiveness that counts today.

We can divide our inner game into four sections: take ownership, use "I" statements, keep things simple and be direct, and don't lead with a compromise.

Take Ownership

Take ownership of the message you want to say. Know what you want to say and how you are going to say it. If you want to tell somebody that you feel hurt because they don't respect your no, plan the words you want to use. Decide when the right time is to say it and even where you should be.

The message that you want to get across is yours to own, so you decide what is best to say and when. When we start to become more assertive, we are able to take ownership of our own lives.

Use "I" statements

The importance of "I" statements can never be underestimated. "I" statements show others that you take responsibility for your feelings. It shows that you feel strongly about a certain issue and at the same time, it reduces the likelihood of others taking your statement personally. Though the meaning of the following two sentences is the same, the receiver of the message can interpret them very differently. "You make me feel weak when you don't listen to me" puts blame on the other person. "I feel weak when you don't listen to me" is how we take responsibility for our own emotions.

Keep Things Simple and Be Direct

Have you ever noticed that when you keep talking (especially when you are nervous) it is impossible to stop? All of a sudden, your original message is lost in a sea of other words and ideas. Your message hasn't been communicated clearly. Not only this, but it gives the other person time to think of a response to your no. Here are some examples of how to be simple and direct:

- No, thank you

- I'm busy later

- I don't feel like it

- That's not good for me

Don't Lead with a Compromise

By leading with a compromise, you are letting the other person know there is wiggle room and they haven't heard no. If they don't hear a no, they will assume that it is a yes. Offering a compromise is a great way to make sure that things get done and problems are solved, but the compromise comes at the end of your message.

While there are still numerous other emotions that arise when learning how to be assertive, fear and anxiety are the two that tend to hold us back from trying. In the next chapter, we will look at being aware of our emotions and how to handle issues like overthinking and feeling guilty.

CHAPTER 3: SELF-AWARENESS AND CONTROLLING YOUR EMOTIONS AND YOUR MIND

T he funny thing about self-awareness is that we assume it is another skill that we all have. It can't really be that difficult to see ourselves clearly. But with the complexities of the human mind and the degrees of self-awareness, it is understandable some guidance is required.

As we go about our daily lives, we are aware of our thoughts and feelings. We know what makes us feel happy or angry. By now, we can understand the triggers of our fears and anxiety. But we rarely consider whether these thoughts are correct.

Self-awareness is the concept of separating yourself from your feelings and thoughts so that you can analyze each one to decide if this is how you should be thinking/acting/feeling. This self-evaluation requires objectivity and a comparison against our standards rather than simply recognizing emotions.

Being self-aware can help us to be more accepting, to gain confidence, make better decisions, and improve our communication skills. Being able to realistically evaluate yourself in a range of different situations will enhance your experiences. Before we look at how to practice self-awareness, let's look at some of the other emotions we experience or the results of being assertive.

Negative Feedback and Criticism

Winston Churchill felt that criticism was a necessary experience in order for us to be able to learn and grow. He also said that if we have been criticized, it is a good thing, because we have stood up for something we believe in. The project you presented is something you believed in, but when you are criticized or receive negative feedback for your work, it is painful, and you may feel embarrassed, angry, or incompetent.

There are so many reasons for somebody to criticize you. It may well be that they are genuinely trying to help you, but they lack the communication skills to provide constructive criticism.

They might be frustrated because they don't think that you have listened to them completely. The person could have made their own mistakes and are trying to highlight yours to draw attention away from themselves. Of course, it can also just be their own fears, they are insecure, or feel threatened by you.

To deal with negative feedback and criticism in an assertive way, in the first place, you must remain calm and take a deep breath. Consider the criticism and agree with only what you feel is true. Correct the person for their false statements. It is important to respond to the words a person is using and not their tone of voice. You may feel that they are coming across as aggressive or angry, but you can't raise your voice to match theirs. Don't attach yourself to their emotions. If your confidence is knocked or you are hurt, suggest talking a little later on, take a few minutes to process the feedback, and decide how you want to respond.

Negative Thoughts

Whether your negative thoughts come from cognitive distortion or a tendency to look on the darker side of life, it is important that we look at learning how to think more positively. Negative thoughts have a powerful impact on your confidence, your body language, and your tone of voice—all of which are critical for being assertive. The positive belief that you can achieve something is often what will give you the confidence to do it.

It is frustrating when people tell you that you need to be more positive. You know this already, but it is never that simple. It requires cognitive restructuring, which some are able to do alone, and others need help with cognitive-behavioral therapy (CBT).

This process involves the identification of a negative thought, understanding whether or not it is valid, and then replacing it with a more positive image:

The negative thought: Your boss is going to get mad when you say no to giving the presentation this weekend.

Validating the thought: Your boss might be angry, but he can't fire you or force you to do it on your day off. The worst they can do is shout, and that won't last forever.

The positive image: You have dinner and drinks with friends that you will be able to enjoy without the stress of working on a Saturday.

This process sounds super easy, but it will take some time to practice. It is important that you take time to think each stage through and not rush it so that it becomes a more natural habit for you.

Anger

There are two sides to anger. First, we have to learn how to cope with people getting angry with us when we are assertive. Although this is a horrible situation, you can't let it stop you from being assertive. It is likely to make you scared to try, but we have now learned some techniques to cope with our fear.

The most important thing is not to retaliate with anger. This is unlikely because, by nature, we are generally passive people. At the same time, this person has crossed an unacceptable boundary, and you shouldn't allow them to feel that they can behave in this way. Focus on "I" statements such as, "I don't appreciate being spoken to in this manner." Then discuss the matter at a later date.

If you know a person is likely to get angry, it is strongly recommended that you make sure there are other people around when you assert yourself. This will prevent the situation from getting out of hand. While you are still practicing your assertive skills and you know a person gets angry, consider using other forms of communication, like email. You can still assert yourself in writing.

On the other hand, people not respecting our wishes when we express them can lead us to feel angry. We need to deal with this anger so that it doesn't fester, and we end up taking it out on someone else.

Here are some healthy ways to deal with anger:

· Countdown from 10 and focus on your breathing. Flood your mind with calming imagery.

· Identify the emotion behind your anger. Is it because you were humiliated, scared, belittled?

· Visualize your anger. Rather than trying to block it out, imagine it as a separate entity to yourself.

· Find an outlet for your anger—physical exercise, go for a walk, play an instrument, paint, or draw.

· Practice mindfulness and meditation for self-calming and relaxation.

· Try not to join in with negative talk. You might not be the only person your boss has shouted at that day. Joining in might feel like you are letting go of your frustration, but it may well magnify it.

· Be nice to the angry person. It sounds hard, but you can do it. Just because they are unkind doesn't mean that you can't be your usual nice self. Their behavior toward you will change when you are kind.

Whenever the emotion of anger rears its head, the best action is always to delay your response. The ability to control your initial reactions will lead to greater success as you have had time to think the situation through completely. Remember the Marshmallow Test. The child that could resist the powerful urge to eat the marshmallow was later rewarded with two. This control was hard but proved fruitful.

Overthinking

Overthinking doesn't have a powerful psychological term such as "cognitive distortion," nevertheless, it is just as concerning. Overthinking is an action that can take over our minds, making it difficult to focus on anything else. Overthinking leads you to doubt yourself and lowers your self-confidence.

We can divide overthinking into two parts: ruminating and worrying. Ruminating is when we replay a situation over and over in our heads, looking at ways you could have done differently. It leads to regretting things you may or may not have done and blaming yourself for the outcomes.

Worrying is actually very similar to cognitive distortion. It is thinking about how a situation is going to play out and the negative things that may happen.

By engaging your brain in a different activity, you should be able to stop the continuous cycle of overthinking. My favorite technique is the elastic band trick. Place an elastic band around your wrist. When you start to notice that you are over-thinking, flick the band—not enough to cause you pain, it's not a punishment. Repeat the words, "Thoughts are not facts." This is a method of reconditioning our thought process.

It is also a good idea to create a limit on the time you allow yourself to make decisions. Start with the smaller choices in life. For example, what to have for dinner. Rather than over-thinking what to eat, allow yourself five minutes. This teaches your brain that you have a limited time to think.

It might be worth keeping a few Post-It notes. If we use the same example as deciding what to eat, you could put a Post-It on the fridge saying, "Am I overthinking?" as this will remind you of the habit of overthinking.

Finally, take a look at the people in your social life. Do you tend to hang out with people who think too much, or are they excellent at keeping things straight? Spend more time with the second group of people so you can learn from them.

Feeling Guilty

It is a massive issue for a people pleaser to be able to say no without feeling guilty. The idea of putting our own needs before others makes us feel selfish, which leads to guilt. There is no magic trick that will stop you from feeling guilty. It goes back to being a nice person and wanting to make others happy.

When it comes to being assertive, remember what guilt actually is. Guilt is the feeling that we have done something wrong. Being assertive is not doing anything wrong, nor is putting your needs before others. We are talking about doing what is right for you. Saying no to something so that you can take care of yourself is nothing to feel guilty about. This is your right, just as it is everyone else's right.

To stop feeling guilty, it is essential that you have your boundaries in place. Decide what behaviors are acceptable for you and what aren't. If you are not comfortable with your friend laughing about your cooking, explain how you feel. Perhaps they didn't know that their teasing upset you. Once they are aware of it, you can assert yourself without feeling guilty because they know your boundaries.

Emotions Management

Emotional management is a strategy that helps us to keep our emotions in check. Without it, it is easy for our negative emotions like anger and pride to take control over our common sense and intelligence.

To be able to manage our emotions, it is necessary for us to stay in the present rather than looking back at past experiences and how they turned out.

Keeping your mind on the emotions you feel in the present prevents you from switching to autopilot, which keeps you attached to past emotions.

Try not to label emotions as good and bad or positive and negative. Not everything is so black and white. When we label emotions, we could end up labeling the situation as the same.

When you have the ability to see the bigger picture, you will notice that every situation has a mixture of different emotions, all of which we can learn from.

Whenever you feel a sudden rush of emotion, it is amazing how taking a step back can be so beneficial. The appearance of a huge wave of feelings leads us to immediately judge ourselves, and more often than not, we judge ourselves too harshly.

Taking a step back allows us a moment to settle our minds and not to act on misguided impulses.

As emotional management is closely related to stepping back from our feelings and being an observer as we do in self-awareness, let's take a closer look at a complete strategy.

How to Practice Self-Awareness and Emotional Control

1. Create time and space for yourself

There is constant daily stress in our lives. From the moment we wake up to the time we fall asleep, our brains are extremely active. If we don't take some time to observe our feelings and emotions, it simply won't happen.

Find a moment each day when you can be alone to connect with yourself, even if it is just a few minutes.

2. Practice mindfulness

Mindfulness enables you to be more aware of your inner-self and how you react to people and situations. Concentrate on what is happening in the moment rather than letting your mind drift from the past to the present.

Focus on your breathing, the sights, sounds, and smells that you notice. You can also practice mindfulness while you are walking, even eating, so it is easy to incorporate into your daily routine.

3. Ask for people's feedback

Those who love you will be able to give you honest feedback about your emotions, maybe even things you hadn't noticed yourself. Talking to others gives you a different perspective on things, opportunities to learn and improve yourself, which in turn, will provide you with more confidence.

4. Keep a journal

Writing your emotions and thoughts down in a journal is an ideal way to process your thoughts. Some people are not comfortable with talking about their emotions with others, and so a journal can give you the chance to express yourself openly without worrying about what other people think.

5. Listen to others

Listening to others and watching how people interact will help you to learn not only what to do, but what not to do. You will also be able to observe body language along with vocabulary and expressions. There is no need to judge or evaluate other people's communication, just watch.

In the first few chapters, we have mentioned the importance of confidence when asserting ourselves. In the next chapter, it's time to start understanding the difference between self-esteem and confidence, and some important techniques to boost both.

CHAPTER 4: BOOSTING YOUR CONFIDENCE

I t's understandable why confidence and self-esteem are often used as synonyms. Both are associated with discovering the courage to achieve the things we want in our life, our goals, and our dreams. Having one doesn't imply that the other will follow.

You can be confident in your skills at work but still not view yourself in a positive way in other areas of your life.

Confidence is having faith in your own abilities. It is deciding what you want to do and knowing that you have the talent and skills to carry it out. Self-esteem is the way we view ourselves and others and our interactions with the world. Those who have a good sense of self-esteem tend to be confident.

In this chapter, we are going to work on methods to improve your self-esteem and your confidence. This way, you will be equipped with knowing how to be assertive and the right way to say no, but you will also have the confidence to be able to speak up for yourself.

How to Improve Your Self-Esteem

At some point, it is normal that we view ourselves negatively. There are so many things that can lead us to having low self-esteem.

Weight is a huge issue for so many and we underestimate the effect on our self-esteem.

Feeling overweight can make us feel uncomfortable in social situations since we unnecessarily compare ourselves to other people, particularly celebrities. This can stop us from enjoying many aspects of our life, from eating a nice meal to having sex.

We might worry about how others view us, not just physically, but the type of person we are. It can be unnerving to think that your behavior isn't considered the cultural norm. You may feel that you don't belong in a certain social group.

Having a low-self-esteem can bring about physical and mental health issues. Our concerns with body image are strongly linked to eating disorders. You may also experience anxiety and depression.

Changing the way you view yourself can seem like an uphill challenge, but it is one that can be done in small steps.

Each little thing you manage to adjust will start to make great differences.

Let's look at some now.

1. Be kind to yourself

There is a little voice inside of you that is feeding your mind with negative thoughts. It is time to put this voice on a leash and encourage a new voice that will counteract the negatives.

Each morning, tell yourself something positive. It doesn't have to be huge.

For example, I have lovely shiny hair, I like my calf muscles, I know a lot about this subject or that, etc. The next day, think of something different. Keep a notebook next to your bed and start making a list.

2. Remind yourself that nobody is perfect

It is simply impossible. Even Mary Poppins was "practically" perfect in every way. The only difference is that some people are better at hiding their flaws than others.

Your goal should never be to become perfect, rather you are looking to improve.

3. Mistakes are part of everyone's life

We don't forget to buy milk or send that important email on purpose. We don't wake up in the morning and say, "Gosh, I hope I make mistakes today." Errors happen! Those with low self-esteem tend to dwell on their mistakes.

Unfortunately, while thinking about what we did wrong, we aren't concentrating on the task at hand and are likely to make more mistakes. The best thing to do is admit your mistake, take responsibility, apologize, and put it behind you.

4. Make time for yourself

Not so that you can catch up on the housework or work your way through your inbox, but to do something you love doing. Regardless of your gender, if a hot bubbly bath with some nice music and a few candles is what you want to do, you should do it. Allow yourself to be happy.

5. Stop comparing yourself to others

Yes, her stomach might be flatter, and his six-pack might be firmer, but that doesn't define who someone is or mean they have a better life. Either one of these people could be in an abusive relationship or have a sick family member.

If you feel envious of what other people have, try complimenting them on it. Being nice to others is a good way to build your self-esteem.

6. With regards to body image

We human beings come in all shapes and sizes, and we are beautiful in our own, individual ways. Take a few minutes to listen to Baz Luhrmann's "Everybody's Free (To Wear Sunscreen)" song. He offers some insightful advice.

In particular, "Enjoy your body; use it every way you can. Don't be afraid of it or what other people think of it. It's the greatest instrument you'll ever own."

Boosting Your Self-Confidence

You will start to notice improvements with your self-confidence when you see yourself in a more positive light after working on the steps to develop your self-esteem.

As our confidence is related to the doubts we have of our own abilities, there are alternative things that will show you just how capable you really are.

1. Brush your hair, shower, shave, and get dressed

Not wishing to insult your intelligence but these simple acts as part of your morning routine will allow you to start the day feeling better about yourself. I once asked my girlfriend why she had to shave her legs before putting on trousers since it's not like anyone will know, and she responded, "But I'll know." Choose outfits that make you feel good.

2. Be prepared

Unknown situations make us doubt whether we have the ability to succeed or not. Perhaps you have to run a meeting or meet new business partners—whatever the situation is— prepare yourself as much as possible. Know what you are going to say, anticipate questions, research locations before you go there. Being prepared will calm your nerves and allow you to feel more confident.

3. Act positively

We have already worked on thinking positively, now it is time to act the same way. Respond to other people's negatives in a positive way and look for the good in every situation.

Even doing things with more energy will help you to act positively. As well as revising your own positivity, make sure to surround yourself with people who are also positive as this will boost your mood.

4. Choose your company wisely

We need to surround ourselves with like-minded, positive, and confident people. Their energy will rub off on you as you get caught up in the atmosphere of a can-do attitude.

On the other hand, try to distance yourself from those who tell you that you can't do something, at least until you have gained more confidence.

5. Set goals and break them down into smaller achievable ones

Setting goals and not reaching them damages confidence. When we don't reach them, it isn't because we aren't capable. It's because we haven't made them into manageable goals.

By breaking down a big goal, you gain momentum each time you achieve a smaller one, reinforcing the fact that you can do it.

6. Learn something every day

We have heard this before, and there is a reason why it is repeated to us. Learning is a wonderful way to empower yourself. It gives you the confidence to join in with conversations and to try new things. While it doesn't have to literally be every day, your learning should be continuous.

7. Clear the clutter from your life

It could be your desk, your kitchen, your entire, home but start having a good clear out. When things become less chaotic, you feel that you have more control over your life.

8. Challenge yourself

There are always things that we want to do but don't feel like we can for one reason or another. It could be running that extra mile, driving in an unfamiliar city, going on a date, as some examples. Don't set yourself up for failure by trying to climb Everest. Find a small action to overcome and triumph at. If you want to go on a date, start by creating a profile on an online dating site rather than walking up to the next person you see and asking them to dinner. Each small win will give you a new burst of confidence

9. Look at your strengths

Those who lack confidence will often spend too much time focusing on the things that they aren't good at and where they need to improve. To boost your confidence, look back at what you have accomplished in your life. What strengths led you to achieve this? This is a reminder of all that you should be proud and confident about.

10. Appreciate your limitations

We don't all have the ability to run a company or to look after five kids at once. Some people can't drive in a city. Whatever your limitations are, know that by creating goals and smaller action plans, you will be able to work toward surpassing your limitations.

11. Work on your body language

Standing up straight and looking at people straight on will help you to feel and appear confident. Don't forget the importance of a smile. Smiling makes the other person feel good, and they are more likely to return the smile, making you feel even better.

12. Take care of yourself

The right diet, amount of sleep, and exercise are essential for not only your body and mind, but also for giving you the necessary energy to cope with the challenges of life and those associated with people pleasing.

Building Up Your Confidence so that You Can Say No

Imagine your self-esteem and confidence as a trickling tap into a bucket. Each drop will make a difference and surprisingly, your bucket will soon fill up. The more techniques that you practice, the faster the water will flow and the sooner you will see the results.

The methods we have discussed to build our self-esteem and confidence will help us when it comes to saying no. We will finish off this chapter by adopting some of the techniques that can help you to confidently say no.

1. Plan what you want to say

Having a plan of what to say will allow you to start the conversation with more confidence. It doesn't have to be a long speech, and a short, simple sentence is enough. But make sure you have thought about what you will say if the person doesn't accept your no the first time.

2. Your no doesn't have to be perfect straight away

We are still learning and the conversation you had in mind might not pan out perfectly, but this is okay. Don't punish yourself if it isn't perfect. Rather look at what you can improve on.

3. Be energetic and positive in your behavior

Acting like Eeyore, the donkey character from Winnie-the-Pooh, won't motivate the other person. It is much harder for them to not accept your no when you have a positive attitude as it will be infectious. Being positive will help the conversation flow in the same manner where you can find alternative solutions.

4. Don't back down

The fastest way to end the discomfort of the situation is to say yes. However, this is going to have a horrible effect on your confidence. If you feel your confidence is wavering, ask for more time, and use the magic words "I will get back to you."

5. Practice saying no to those who fill you with confidence

There are some people who will accept your no as if nothing had ever happened. These are the people that you want to practice saying no to. It will give you the opportunity to experiment with all that you have learned and master your skills.

6. Celebrate your wins

Though it might seem small to some people, you have overcome a giant hurdle in your life, and this needs to be rewarded. Treat yourself to a bar of chocolate, a cold beer, or the new jeans you wanted. Take a moment to appreciate your achievement.

One thing that I remind myself and my clients is that it is also okay if your confidence is knocked a little. The most important thing is that we are improving and moving forward. A small step back doesn't mean we are back to square one, and it certainly doesn't mean that you will never be able to assert yourself. If you are learning how to speak a new language you will make mistakes with the odd word or pronunciation, but you are always getting better. These mistakes help you to learn even faster. The same theory can be applied to learning how to be assertive.

In the next chapter, we are going to explore how our surrounding and life habits can impact our ability to be assertive.

CHAPTER 5: WHAT HABITS AND PRACTICES CAN WE CHANGE IN OUR LIVES TO BE MORE ASSERTIVE?

Deciding that we want to become more assertive and standing up for our beliefs will often lead us to look at what needs to be changed on the inside. Naturally, we will have to find more confidence and develop better communication skills. Nevertheless, there are other things that we can do to make the process easier. To an extent, we can call these the physical or more tangible changes that we would like to see a difference in alongside the emotional changes.

Understanding and Developing Your Needs

You will find it difficult to assert yourself if you are unclear on what exactly your needs are. Your needs can be physical and emotional. It is possible that you need to feel more respected or you need to feel more love in your relationship. Some people need physical contact to feel that love, such as hand-holding and hugs. Personally, I can't cope without time alone, and it is probably my biggest need. Everyone's needs will be very different.

As adults, we have the knowledge and experience to meet our needs, but only when we are able to pinpoint what they are exactly. Each need is attached to or brings about a certain feeling, and we need to keep analyzing the need until we get to the feeling. This is called the "onion peeling process" in which we take back the layers until we get to the source of our needs. How do you feel when your needs are met? When I am alone, I initially feel overwhelmed with all I need to do before the house is full again. Then I have a rush of energy while getting everything done. The final layer of my metaphorical onion is a huge wave of peace and calm. Now, I have identified my need.

When developing your needs, you need to carve out some time and space for yourself. This is going to be the hardest part because you will always feel like there is someone or something that deserves this time more than you do. Every excuse not to allow yourself some time is like a baseball flying toward you. Make sure you hit those baseballs out of the park until you have no excuses left.

Setting Goals

You can call them goals, dreams, heart's desires, bucket list—there are so many words for what are essentially the things that we want to achieve. We will have massive long-term goals, such as buying a house or traveling around another country. We will have mid-term goals, perhaps moving up the career ladder, and short-term goals that we would like to achieve in the next six to twelve months. For those of us who write daily to-do lists, they are still a form of a goal.

Goals are crucial for everyone since they provide us with the motivation to keep trying and working hard. They encourage us to learn more, and they help us develop as a person. They give us moments to celebrate.

Your goals can be related to becoming more assertive. We would break this down into smaller steps, so instead of coming straight out with a no, our initial goal would be to tell someone that you would think about it. Our goal might be to become healthier, so we would start by reducing fatty foods before jumping straight into the kale smoothies and one-hour spinning class. In order to spend a month in Australia, you will need to save money, so you could break this down into saving for flights, saving for accommodation, etc.

Once each goal is broken down into smaller steps, you need to devise a plan to achieve each one. So, if we wanted to become healthier, our first goal could be achieved if in the first week we cut out sweets and chocolate, the second week fried foods, the third week processed foods, and so on.

All goals, the steps to reaching the goal, and the plan to achieve each one, has to be written down. You should also share your goals with as many people as possible. This way, they become real, and you are held accountable for them. If John woke up and wanted to paint his living room that day but didn't write it down or tell his wife, there is no evidence of his goal. If he doesn't achieve it, no one has to know. If he told his wife, she would be able to encourage him throughout the day, and he would have the great satisfaction of crossing off all that he had succeeded in doing.

Changing Your Habits

These are not all but some of the likely habits a non-assertive person may have:

• They don't point out socially rude behavior, queue hopping, arriving late, talking with your mouth full

• They won't start a conversation

• When invited into a conversation, they will tend to agree with the crowd rather than voice their own opinion

• They won't ask questions for fear of feeling stupid

• They can be emotionally dishonest

• They find it very difficult to accept a compliment

• Their voice may be weak, shaky, or too quiet

• They will struggle to make eye contact

• They have nervous habits like nail-biting, fiddling with hair, pen clicking

• It is hard for them to genuinely smile, but it's more like a nervous grin

Let's start by making a list of five or six habits that you have. Identify the situation that causes these habits. Now write down how you would like to see yourself react when these habits appear. Work on changing one habit at a time. There is no need to put pressure on yourself to change too many things at once.

Adapting Your Surroundings

It's not likely that you would make a connection between your surroundings and your ability to assert yourself until you connect the dots. To be assertive, you need to have self-esteem and confidence. For this, you need to be happy and to love yourself, and this requires you to take care of yourself and be grateful.

Make a list of things that you would like to change about your home. Perhaps a decent spring cleaning and decluttering will allow you to feel better about your home, or you might want to start painting some of the rooms and redecorating. If you are not satisfied with your full-time job, you might consider taking some courses to improve your resumé before you look for a new environment.

The people you surround yourself with is also crucial at this point. There are some people in your life that make you feel bad about yourself, whether intentional or unintentional. Others can be too overpowering and will struggle to accept the changes you want to make in your life.

You should try to distance yourself from these people and protect your surroundings from their negativity. These people may harm your progress in the early stages. That's not to say you should remove them from your life completely. It is a case of putting some space between you and them while you become stronger and more confident in your ability to assert yourself.

How to Determine Your Boundaries

Boundaries are a little bit like needs, and it can be hard to put your finger on them. Quite often, you won't realize that you have a certain boundary until it has been crossed, as you won't know how you truly feel until you are in that situation. When you are considering your boundaries, try to determine what is your absolute no.

Take social media as an example. We could consider the following boundaries:

• I am happy to have a social media account but not post on it

• I am comfortable with other people posting about me on their social media pages

• I draw the line at people posting photos of me on social media

As we said, you might not appreciate how violated you feel until you see a photo of yourself online. It is difficult to be mad at the person who posted it, because if you didn't realize how you would feel, then how would the person who posted it know?

Because boundaries are personal and there are so many possibilities, it is impossible to compile a list. There are five categories of boundaries that you can explore:

• **Physical boundaries:** your body, your personal space

•**Emotional boundaries:** being in touch with your feelings

• **Sexual boundaries:** what is okay and what is off-limits

- **Intellectual boundaries:** respect for different opinions, beliefs, cultures

- **Financial boundaries:** not being the person who always pays, when to lend money and when not to

A good exercise is to look back over the last year or two and examine the situations that have hurt you, upset you, or made you feel angry. It is probably because someone has overstepped a boundary, but you have never put a name to it. Don't forget that boundaries will apply to your relationships at work, friendships, partner, and family.

Before you start writing a list of all the habits and practices that you want to change, let's remember that Rome wasn't built in a day, and we don't have to do everything at once. When you have completed the list, look at the things you can do this week, this month, and in the next three months. If you want the changes to last, it is better to put all of your effort into them, which may take more than 24 hours!

So far, we have worked hard on making changes that will make us happy and enjoy our lives more. We can feel ourselves becoming more confident, and we know what we want to do and how we want to do it. It's time to start putting all of this into action and be assertive.

CHAPTER 6: ASSERTIVENESS – YOUR WORDS AND YOUR ACTIONS

This chapter is going to pack a punch, and I hope that at the end of it, though you won't believe me just yet, you are going to feel motivated to get out there and assert yourself, maybe even a little bit excited!

Assertive Statements for Multiple Situations

In some situations, our goal is to say no, so let's tackle this first. The statements we are going to look at are all related to somebody asking us to do something that we don't want to do. It is more than likely that they are going to be expecting you to say yes. Over the years, people became so used to me saying yes that I found they wouldn't even bother waiting for an answer.

The first set of basic no statements are all about creating empathy and understanding, which is why we soften the assertive statement with a "Thank you." If you want to increase the amount of empathy, you can use some of the longer assertive statements.

- Thanks, but I don't have the time.

- Thanks, but I have other plans.

- Thanks, but I'm not interested.

- Thank you for thinking of me, but I am going to have to say no this time.

- Thanks for letting me know, but I won't be able to make it.

- Thank you for considering me, but I am too busy right now.

The next set of statements will give you more time to decide whether you want to do something or not. Or they will allow you to prepare yourself more for saying no.

- I have a lot on my mind right now, so I am going to take some time to think about it.

- Let me sleep on it.

- I'm not sure, I will get back to you.

- Once I have finished this task, I will consider it.

- Can I get back to you on that tomorrow/later in the day?

We use "I" statements to clearly express how we feel or what our thoughts are on a matter. Remember, avoid starting with "You" because it may come across as a personal attack.

- I can see where you are coming from, but I don't agree.

- I feel disrespected when you interrupt me/laugh at my opinions/ignore me.

- I take offense at what you have said.

- I would like it if you allowed me to share my views.

- I don't like being shouted at in that way.

- I am uncomfortable with your tone of voice/language.

Then building up to assertive statements that include the word no. Again, you can keep it very short or soften it up if you prefer.

- No.

- Absolutely not.

- No, thank you.

- No, not today.

- Thanks, but no thanks.

- No, I have another commitment.

- No, it's not possible today.

Although it has been said before, you have the right to use any of these assertive statements. As long as you do so in the right way, without coming across as aggressive, keep telling yourself that you are doing nothing wrong.

Assertive Body Language

Psychologists and experts may disagree on this. Some people will tell you to "fake it till you make it." This idea means that although you don't feel confident, you act as if you are by focusing on assertive body language. Others will say that once you begin to feel more confident, your body language will naturally show this. Both can be true, which is why I encourage people to work on both.

You might begin an assertive conversation feeling confident but start to lose some of this confidence halfway through. It is amazing how shifting your body language can still help you to appear confident. On the other hand, we can't rely on body language alone. Our journey to improving ourselves is dependent on feeling confident so that we can become assertive. For this, we will look at assertive body language, but not to replace our confidence, so that we are aware of it and can use it as a tool along with our techniques.

• Stand up straight, don't hunch your shoulders.

• Keep your hands where they can be seen. Hands behind your back suggest you are hiding something. Open palms imply that you are being open.

• Look straight at the person who is talking.

• Make a comfortable amount of eye contact.

• Don't let your eyes dart all over the room. It implies you are nervous.

• Speak loud enough to be heard clearly, but don't shout.

• Speak slowly, keep your voice steady, and don't hesitate.

• Keep your facial expressions gentle and offer an honest smile.

Practicing in the mirror really does give you the chance to learn more about your body language and how these small changes come across and make a difference. I always recommend practicing body language with a trusted friend too.

Here you can find a video with five exercises to do at home that will improve your posture. They will be able to tell you when your smile looks real, and when you look like you are just suffering.

Scan the QR code above to open the video with five exercises.

If you can't open it, please use this short link:

http://bit.ly/5exer

Yoga is an amazing practice to improve your posture. Not only that but you can do a few poses in the morning without taking up too much of your time and start the day fresh.

Daily Yoga is one of the best free yoga apps out there right now. If you wanted to, you could also join a class as there are so many for different levels, types, and times of the day. It's a nice way to meet like-minded people.

Practical Skills to Increase Your Assertiveness

Effective communication is about more than the words you say and the body language you use. Here, we can see practical methods to improve assertive skills when looking at the bigger picture.

Verbal Skills

Verbal skills include the words we use, our sentence structure, and the ability to use the right adjectives to accurately describe how you are feeling. To have good verbal communication skills, you need to be able to express empathy and know when to give credit when credit is due.

Tips:

• Expand your vocabulary. When you think of how you feel, use a thesaurus to look up synonyms and antonyms.

• Use expressions that start with "I understand."

• Keep your tone varied so that you engage your listener.

• Stay on topic. Beating around the bush or talking about things that aren't relevant may confuse your audience.

Listening Skills

People rarely listen enough to what the other person is saying. It is harder for us because we are concentrating so much on being assertive that we can be distracted from what is being said. It's about being able to interpret the message that is being sent.

Tips:

• Show people that you are listening by repeating parts of what has been said.

• Never make judgments about what the other people are saying.

• Make sure you are facing your audience.

•Don't assume the other person wants or needs your opinion.

Social Skills

Any social situation is a potential nightmare for those who struggle to assert themselves. It is difficult to join in with conversations when we fear what others think about us. Social skills are not based on intelligence but rather on the ability to interact with others in various settings.

Tips:

• Ask open-ended questions that lead to new conversations instead of yes/no questions.

An ***open-ended question*** *is a question that cannot be answered with a "yes" or "no".*

Example: *Why did you choose that restaurant?*

- Brush up on your small talk conversation, latest films, restaurants, the location you are in, hobbies, and try not to resort to the weather.

- Compliment others, whether it's their clothes, their ideas, and the way they interact with others.

- Encourage others to talk about themselves and what they like so that you can find things in common.

Saying No

One of the biggest mistakes we tend to make when saying no in an assertive way is to talk too much. We start to offer explanations as to why we can't do something. This weakens our positions. The longer we talk, the longer we have to start feeling guilty and we can even manage to talk ourselves out of our own decision. Many times, it's not even necessary as the person will accept our no.

Tips:

- Prepare your answer, make sure it is short and simple, and be prepared to say no again and again.

- Keep a mental image of what you will be doing in the time that you aren't doing something that you don't want to do. Fill your mind with this instead of feeling like you are a bad person for saying no.

- Be polite, but don't feel the need to apologize for your decision.

- If necessary, tell them you will think about it, but don't feel pressured into saying yes.

Set Boundaries:

When people learn about your boundaries as they come up, you often reduce the need to assert yourself. If our friend is aware that they can't post photos of us online, they shouldn't do it. Because you have already told them that you aren't comfortable, it is much easier for you to assert your feelings when they do.

Tips:

• Know what your boundaries are, and be clear about your limits.

• If someone tests or pushes your boundaries, put a stop to it right away. Use "I" sentences to let them know why you have set your boundaries.

• Respect other people's boundaries, and if you aren't sure, ask beforehand. For example, don't go to hug or kiss a stranger on the cheek unless you know they are comfortable with it.

• Never allow someone to cross your boundaries. Doing so is a sign of disrespect, and they will only do it again and again.

Because of the sheer scope of situations, we are going to start taking a closer look at the different types of relationships we have, and we are now going to examine our assertive behavior within each. As you can imagine, being assertive with your boss isn't the same as being assertive with your parents. Firstly, let's talk about our personal relationships and discover how we can achieve what we want without hurting our loved one's feelings.

CHAPTER 7: LEARNING HOW TO BE ASSERTIVE IN OUR PERSONAL RELATIONSHIPS

O ur personal relationships involve a massive range of emotions before we even consider being assertive.

We have friends that we like, friends that we love, partners who we can't live without, even when they drive us crazy, and our family, which we can love, hate, and everything in between.

These are the people in our life who we least want to hurt and disappoint. Their opinion matters more than anyone else's in the world, as does their happiness.

Asserting yourself within personal relationships can, to an extent, be easier because we may have more confidence with these people.

At the same time, our need to please them can make it even more complicated.

Rest assured, there are manageable solutions to begin standing up for yourself. Let's start by examining our friendships.

Being Assertive with Your Friends

There are two types of friendships to consider: the old gang of friends you have known for years, and those that are still relatively new friends. The new friends are the absolute ideal people to begin your assertiveness with. You have overcome the initial awkwardness and know that they are someone you want in your life. However, they still don't know you very well.

With your new friends, it is essential that you start with a clean slate. They don't know you are not an assertive person or that you struggle saying no.

By now, you should have your boundaries clear in your mind, and it is easier to introduce into your friendship from day one. Don't feel that you have to wait for them to do this. You might find that once you start clearly defining what you are comfortable with and where you draw the line, they will do the same.

The result of this is a wonderful, open, and honest friendship built on trust and respect. You may even find that because of this, your friendship will become stronger than some that you already have. After all, in their eyes, you aren't doing anything out of the ordinary.

With friendships that have lasted a while, there are certain steps you can take to help you first understand where the problem is coming from so that you can then work toward the solutions.

1. Assess your friendships

You may feel like your opinions aren't valued. It could be that you feel left out of conversations, or that you are the one who is always checking up on the other person. Perhaps you make plans together, but the other person is always canceling on you.

Look back over situations where you have felt disappointed by your friends. What exactly sparked your feelings?

2. Keep a journal of your feelings

This will help you to keep track of the different circumstances where you should be asserting yourself. You will see patterns in the relationship that need to be stopped.

It will also provide you with a chance to process your feelings. Not just understand why you are feeling hurt but the when and why behind it.

Keeping a journal also helps you to brainstorm potential ideas to solve the problems.

3. Talk to your friends about how you are feeling.

You don't have to see this step as being assertive, even though, to an extent, you are. If you start to build it up to be a huge conversation, you are likely to stress yourself out.

Instead, make it a chat over coffee or a drink, something casual. Explain how you have been feeling and the changes you would like to see.

4. Discover ways that you can improve your relationship together.

Maybe there is a new activity you could sign up for together, something that you want to do rather than what they prefer.

5. If the behavior you don't like continues, it is time to be more assertive.

But now that you have had the initial conversation, it will be easier for you. You can tell your friend that you have already discussed this, and you made it clear how you felt. Be firm with your friends, and use stronger adjectives to describe your emotions. Instead of the word angry, you can use furious.

6. If your friend continues to ignore you, it could be a sign that it is time to rethink the friendship.

This might sound harder than being assertive, but if they are unwilling to see your point of view after you have clearly expressed yourself, it is unlikely that they are going to change. Remember that ignoring you is a sign of passive-aggressive behavior, and this is their problem, not something that you should have to settle for.

7. Look at building new friendships.

While you distance yourself from friends who don't respect you, you have a chance to meet new ones. Sign up for a new sports class or other activities you enjoy. It is possible that you meet people here that share other interests you have.

It's very rare that a true friend won't listen to how you are feeling and make a great effort to fix the wrong. There is no need to assume that you are about to lose all of your friends. Nevertheless, even the best of friendships don't always stand the test of time.

Consider if you are better off having this person in your life and being unhappy, or finding new friends.

With family, this is not quite as simple.

When Your Family Struggle to Appreciate Your Assertiveness

You are certainly not the only person who has made mistakes when communicating with their family. It is possible that you have had moments when you have been passive and then felt like you have been walked over. In a moment of rage, you may have shouted and felt awful afterward.

Being assertive with our family has major benefits, not just for you, but also for them. It allows us to reduce the tension in stressful situations.

Instead of either party becoming frustrated and displaying negative emotions, they are able to express themselves calmly. This way, communication is enhanced. Everyone involved is able to better understand their feelings and the feelings of others.

Being assertive with your family is more about successful communication than it is about you asserting yourself, or at least in the beginning. Here are some suggestions on how to improve communication within a family.

Try not to make comparisons

When you compare your children or yourself with other family members, you are encouraging a sense of competitiveness that can lead to lowering self-esteem and confidence. Asserting yourself is about celebrating individuality and that it's okay to be different.

Show your understanding

Mutual respect is necessary if you want to be able to assert yourself.

It is important that you try to understand family members' feelings and show empathy toward them. Take time to listen to how each other feels.

Be clear about what you are saying

Quite often, we will ask questions that are aimed at what you think others want to do, for example, "Would you like to go out for dinner?" The suggestion implies that you want to go out for dinner, but this is not clear.

Instead, you should say "I would like to go out for dinner." It's probable that your family member will want to join you, and you are not left feeling disappointed.

Do not waffle

When we start to talk too much, we come across as insecure, and the impact of your assertiveness is lost.

Keep in mind some short, precise assertive statements that we have practiced and work at sticking to them.

Be completely honest with your family

Your body has a habit of revealing what you aren't saying. Your words may say one thing, but your body language will display how you truly feel.

When telling white lies to spare the feelings of others, you are sending mixed signals, which will confuse your message.

What to Do When Your Family Ignores Your Assertive Behavior

The most common situations are with parents who don't respect our ability to make our own decisions and stand up for ourselves. We call this "toxic love." It may seem that they are still treating us like children and don't trust us to make our own way in the world. This can hurt because by now, as a successful adult, they should be able to trust your decision-making abilities. The problem is, when they second-guess your choices or opinions, you start to second-guess yourself and start to feel guilty.

As part of learning, specifically about communication, we have looked at trying to understand the other person's feelings. While you may have been angry in the past because of this controlling behavior, it's necessary to take a step back and consider how your parents are feeling. In rare cases, parents are trying to manipulate you, which we will discuss in a minute. However, it's most common that your parents are just scared. They are scared that you will get hurt or make mistakes, and it is natural for a parent to want to protect their adult child. They may also be scared of being left alone as you venture further into the world. This may sound ridiculous if you are in your 30s or 40s, but the older they get, the more they feel they will need you and want to keep you closer.

When you see your parents as scared, rather than controlling, it is not so easy to get angry, and you will find it easier to talk to them as the empathy kicks in.

For many clients and I, it has been more beneficial to actually speak more than our usual short assertive statements. You can explain how you have come to your decisions or opinions, and this shows them that you have thought about each step in detail. Knowing that you have covered all possibilities will help them to see that you haven't just made a random choice.

Manipulation requires a firm hand. There may still be some fear behind a manipulative person, but it's unforgivable because they have taken your assertiveness, considered it, but chosen tactics like guilt and shame to get what they want. They will make you feel like you don't care about them. Regardless of which family member it is, the first thing you might need to do is calm down and distance yourself from the situation.

• Look at the whole picture — their manipulation tactics might be because they are looking out for themselves and just being selfish. They might also just want to spend time with you but are going about it the wrong way. Getting down to the bottom of their manipulation will help you determine how you respond.

• Ask for more information about their request—if the bigger picture is not clear, ask some questions. When your dad asks you to come over to help him, find out what he needs help with. A simple job request could mean he just wants to see you, or your mom has put him up to it. If he genuinely needs help, you can decide if you can or can't.

• If you feel that you are being manipulated, use "I" statements to clearly express your feelings without insulting them.

"I don't like it when I feel obligated to do something that I don't want to do."

• Don't allow interruptions. Aside from a lack of respect, not allowing you to finish sentences and interrupting you are both signs of invalidating your feelings. Try not to interrupt them to tell them that you don't like being interrupted, as it's a bit of a pot calling the kettle black scenario. "Please don't interrupt me" is all you should have to say to get your point across.

If you have been able to express how you feel and your family member has listened and taken everything on board, you should feel that you are more respected from here on. You might need an assertive reminder every once in a while, for example, "Mom, we have talked about how I feel when you insist I do something," but it shouldn't require any acts of assertiveness that leads you to feel uncomfortable or fearful.

Unfortunately, there will be times when people continue to ignore you. Unlike your friends, it is not as simple to distance yourself from them. You have to assert yourself if you want to have a happy, loving relationship with your family.

Have a stern talk to yourself. There is no need to be angry with yourself as you still haven't done anything wrong. But you do need to tell yourself that you have set boundaries with your family. You have reminded them of those boundaries, yet they continue to ignore you. Being firm with yourself will strengthen your beliefs that you are in the right to ask for what you want.

If family members keep insisting that you do things that you don't want to do, and you have already used assertive statements with empathy ("Thank you, but no, I have plans"), you will need to use the firm statements or just say no.

Bear in mind that you have been assertive, and you haven't failed. This person's lack of respect requires you to be ultra-assertive. Ultra-assertive statements include the straightforward "no" as well as:

- Stop!

- That's enough.

- I will not tolerate this.

- I said no, and I mean no.

- Because of your lack of respect, I don't want to make plans with you again.

- I cannot respect you when you act like this.

Being ultra-assertive is still not being aggressive. But you may find that your bluntness can cause the other person to become angry. Be firm, tell them that you can talk again once they have calmed down, and walk away. Be proud of your excellent communication skills and the progress you have made.

Letting Your Partner See Your Assertive Side

Partners are both a family member and a friend. You can't hide away from being assertive, after all, you probably spend more time with your partner than you do your friends and family. And you can't give up on your relationship every time you don't feel like they value your thoughts or wishes.

For this reason, we need to use a combination of the techniques we have already talked about with our friends and family. Without repeating it all again, let's make a summary of the assertive behaviors that can be used in relationships.

Have a solid foundation for communication

Don't bottle up your feelings for fear of rocking the boat at home. It is better that you are both able to express how you feel when certain emotions arise rather than waiting until you are at boiling point.

If your partner leaves their dirty dishes everywhere, explain that you don't appreciate it and that both of you should be responsible for taking care of the home.

Take time to listen to them

Understand their point of view. If the phone rang and they forgot, the problem should be resolved, as it was a genuine mistake. Continuing to mention the dirty dishes will only show the other person that you haven't listened and respected what they have said.

Admit to your own mistakes

There will be a time where you forget your dirty dishes, and they do have the right to pick you up on this. Responding with "Well, you left your washing on the floor" is just tick for tack and isn't productive.

Be polite

It sounds basic, but after some time, we get so comfortable and even assume certain things and forget to say please and thank you. Showing gratitude is a part of healthy communication.

Treat each other as equals

Despite being in the 21st century, this is still a big challenge for many couples. Equality is not limited to who does the chores. Be equal with your finances, time, and the right to individual opinions. Compromise and negotiation is the key to equality in a relationship.

Never sacrifice your values or your beliefs, nor apologize for them

Just because you are a couple doesn't mean you have to share values and beliefs. Each of you must be true to what you believe in and respect the differences.

When you need to assert yourself, focus on statements that explain to your partner how you feel rather than making them feel like they are to blame. "I" statements are necessary, so stick to statements that begin with "I feel" rather than "You make me feel."

Separate your emotion from your intention

It is one thing to be aware of your emotions, it is another to allow these emotions to cloud your intention. Your intention is to communicate that you feel angry, and it is not to show them that you are angry.

Do not fear being assertive or even ultra-assertive

We might fear being assertive because of the other person's reaction, but many times, we fear the worst, and that this person will leave us. Being assertive in a relationship can generally lead to one of three things:

1. Your partner learns to respect your beliefs, boundaries, and opinions.

2. The situation may lead to an argument, which is not a bad thing. Healthy conflict clears the air and allows you to express raw emotions.

3. Your relationship may come to an end, not because you asserted yourself, but because your personality types weren't compatible.

It may sound brutal to look at it this way, and there will be varying degrees of both 1, 2, and 3. Try not to think of the worst-case scenario when you are far from it. Being assertive in your relationship isn't looking for a fight. It is simply a form of communication. There is absolutely nothing wrong with people in different types of relationships having different opinions. Life would be quite dull if we all thought and acted in the same way. Rather than disagreeing on differences, embrace them and use them to expand your knowledge.

CHAPTER 8: BEING ASSERTIVE IN YOUR CAREER, REGARDLESS OF YOUR ROLE

Work relationships can be equally complex. We have probably all had colleagues who we see as friends and others we try to avoid at all costs. There are bosses we dread having to deal with and others that we only want to please. When you are the boss, there are even more challenges for the non-assertive to show their assertion.

Just because we don't have a personal relationship with our co-workers, it doesn't mean that we can go through our working day being passive. Due to the long hours that we spend in the workplace, it is paramount that we are able to express ourselves without fear of repercussions so that you can enjoy your time in the office.

As an employee, we tend to go to extremes in order to be the hard-working, reliable person that the boss is looking for. Surely this dedicated behavior is what will lead us to the promotion we desire? Probably not.

Without the ability to say no in the workplace, you end up becoming the person who does all the tasks that nobody else wants to do. If your colleague doesn't want to prepare a presentation, they will ask you. If someone doesn't want to be on call that weekend, they will ask you to do it. Not being able to say no to these additional responsibilities will have a negative impact on our ability to carry out our own tasks and can cause burnout. Not to mention, constantly saying yes to people at work will start to eat into your social life.

There is no difference in the assertiveness you need in your personal relationships as that in your professional relationships. Whether you are the junior clerk or CEO, being assertive at work is about confidently communicating in a respectful manner so that you receive the treatment you and everyone else deserves. You can set individual and team goals but don't feel the need to be pushy about them, and you are able to say no when necessary. All of this is achieved while maintaining positive relationships in the workplace.

Asserting Yourself as an Employee

Asserting yourself in the workplace requires the fundamentals that we have mentioned various times now:

1. Developing your self-esteem and confidence. Recognize your value and what you are good at.

2. Taking a step back to see the complete picture.

3. Analyze whether you want to say yes or no.

4. Prepare short and simple sentences about what you want to say.

5. Use "I" statements to clearly communicate your feelings.

6. Pay attention to your body language by maintaining eye contact, standing up straight, and smiling.

7. Ask for more time if you aren't sure instead of backing down and saying yes under pressure.

8. Be firm with your assertive statements. Don't feel you need to explain yourself or justify your answers.

What does differ from other relationships is that every employee has certain rights in the workplace that they are entitled to. There are legal and ethical boundaries that cannot be crossed. If you find yourself in a position where one of your boundaries is being crossed, it is possible that a legal boundary is also being crossed or a law is being broken. Sexual advances are a classic example, and this doesn't only apply to women. You might feel like a hand on your leg or a rub of the shoulder is crossing the line, others may not, but this could be considered sexual harassment. A staff member who asks you if they can borrow $20 from the cash register is crossing an ethical boundary. Here are some boundaries that should be considered in the workplace:

• Inappropriate language

• Verbal abuse

• Sexual contact

• Sexual advances

• Disclosing personal information

- Breaching confidentiality

- Accepting gifts from clients

- Disrespecting religious or cultural beliefs

You should educate yourself on the legal and ethical boundaries of your workplace as this will empower you and make it easier for you to assert yourself because it is not just your boundaries that are being crossed, it may well be the law.

You should also check your contract so that you know exactly what your legal rights and responsibilities are. If your boss asks you to work through your lunch hour, it is more than possible that they are overstepping a legal boundary. When the law is behind you, it doesn't feel like you are alone in standing up for your rights. You will be able to find all of the information in your employee policy manual.

For people who still find it difficult to assert themselves in the workplace, the other way to look at it is that it might not only be you who is being taken advantage of. If this is a repeated habit, many others will be in exactly the same position as you are.

It isn't your responsibility to fix all of the problems, but the reward you would feel for being the person who asserted themselves and fixed the wrong would be immensely beneficial for your confidence and the respect that others have for you.

Asserting Yourself as a Boss

I was talking to a woman not so long ago. She was in her early 30s and employed a man who was in his late 50s. Generally, their working relationship was good. She knew he was never going to be happy having a woman as his boss, but she quietly accepted this.

In the space of a few weeks, he asked her to help him with some personal administration, was rude to a client, and didn't show up to two meetings without even notifying her. When she mentioned that this behavior was not acceptable, he became angry. She knew at that point that she would have to think outside the box.

The next day after things had calmed down, she invited him to her house (it wasn't the first time, and they had enjoyed some social occasions, so she felt it wasn't inappropriate). She poured him a glass of wine and asked him if he was okay. The man burst into tears and said he thought that he was about to get a severe telling off. They discussed everything that had been happening and resolved all issues.

Obviously, in the majority of cases, this is not a suitable solution for employee-employer relationships. The point is, there are multiple ways for a boss to assert themselves without making employees feel uncomfortable and without coming across as the big bad boss.

Choose your battles

If you are a team leader, it is your role to control the behavior, actions, and results of your team, not the whole office. If you are a manager or director, you should focus your assertion on the team leaders. You should only focus on the bigger problems and not micromanage everyone.

Set clear expectations

Your expectations are like boundaries and include what you will and will not tolerate. These expectations should be displayed in your location, discussed in the interview phase, and incorporated in training sessions. Like boundaries, when someone falls short of the expectations, it is easier to assert yourself to resolve the issue.

Encourage questions

When your team members and/or team leaders are encouraged to ask questions, you are creating an environment that promotes healthy communication. If an employee doesn't fully understand the directions, they will feel more comfortable to ask for clarification, and fewer mistakes are made.

Mirror the body language of your employees

If they are all lifelessly slumped around the table, then no. But, for example, if they are sitting down at the table, then join them instead of remaining standing or pacing around the table as this can be a sign of dominating or aggressive behavior.

Learn how to say no

This again, hey! People assume that it requires no effort for a boss to say no. Even bosses can be people pleasers and have a strong need for their employees to like them. Requests may seem small at first; an employee wants to come in an hour later but work an hour later, and you say yes. All of a sudden, your employees are coming to you every day with schedule requests.

- Assess each request and consider which ones are reasonable and won't have an impact on the rest of the business. Say yes to those that you agree with.

- If you are unsure, tell employees that you will get back to them soon.

- Ask for more information if you aren't able to make a clear decision.

- Be empathetic with your nos. Thank the employee for their contribution. Let them know that although their idea doesn't work now, you will keep it in mind for the future.

- In the unlikely event that an employee becomes insistent, analyze your body language and make adjustments if necessary, mainly, sit up straighter. Use more assertive statements such as "Thank you, but I have already responded to your request."

As an employer, the one area that you cannot afford to not assert yourself in is the legal and ethical boundaries. If anybody comes to you with an issue, regardless of how small it may seem, it has to be addressed immediately. Dealing with it may make you feel uncomfortable, but by using the communication techniques you have learned, you will succeed. And as a little extra motivation, dealing with a potential lawsuit for not addressing the situation will be far more uncomfortable, stressful, and costly than one assertive conversation.

Assertiveness in the workplace is an excellent communication tool that can help resolve conflicts, allow teams to work better together, and increase employee satisfaction. There will still be differences in opinions, and this is to be expected when different personalities are working in such close proximity. Here is one final idea to practice being assertive in the workplace. Go to your boss or team leaders and suggest assertive training for employees!

CHAPTER 9: KNOWING WHEN AND HOW TO SPEAK UP FOR YOURSELF

There are so many instances throughout a day when you have just a few seconds to decide whether or not you should stand up for yourself or not. You worry about being that person who is always being difficult and often feel that it is better to keep quiet.

Have you ever had those moments when you start to say something and then get all flustered and just feel like an idiot?

Then there are the times when you didn't stand up for yourself and then regret it later. I hated reliving conversations in my head thinking "If only I had said that" or "Why didn't I think of that at the time?"

We have talked about the importance of being confident in order to be able to assert yourself. More often than not, this confidence starts by understanding when you should stand up for yourself.

This short chapter is going to focus on learning when you should assert yourself and defend your thoughts and beliefs, along with when you should wait for a better moment.

There are some very clear situations where you have to stand up for yourself in the moment no matter where you are or who you are with.

Any acts of violence, sexual assault, verbal or physical abuse can't be brushed under the rug. Leaving such issues unresolved can have severe long-term effects.

It is essential that you let the person know exactly how you are feeling and that their behavior is not acceptable under any circumstances.

If you do not have the confidence to stand up for yourself in the moment, this is perfectly understandable as even assertive people can be thrown off balance by such violations.

You must, however, seek help so that it can be dealt with correctly.

Go to your superior (or any superior in the workplace), or talk to the police. If you need to ask a friend to go with you to the station, then do that.

For those situations where you aren't sure, follow these simple steps to allow you to make a more informed decision:

1. Is it a good time?

Consider what mood you are both in. Are you tired, or have you already had a bad day? Do you have enough time to have the conversation, or will you be interrupted?

2. Is the person going to fully listen to you?

Can you see that they will be easily distracted? Do you think that they are in the right frame of mind to care about what you are saying? Is it because the time is not right or that they are never going to be able to listen to you?

3. Are you emotionally calm?

If you don't have your feelings under control, then it might be better to hold off. It's important that you can get your message across without getting upset or angry.

4. Decide what has caused you to feel upset, angry, or frustrated

Pinpoint the reason why you are feeling the way you are so that you are able to effectively communicate this with the other person.

5. Could you be more confident at another moment?

When we learn more about a situation, we often feel more confident. Do you think that this is a situation that you could learn more about and address at another time with more knowledge and confidence?

6. Think about whether there is room for flexibility

Somebody wants you to do something, and you don't want to do it. One person voices their opinion, and yours is different. Is there room for alternatives, common ground, or coming to an agreement? If the answer is no, there might be a better time for the conversation.

How to Stand Up for Yourself

Once you have decided it is the right time to stand up for yourself, it is all about sticking to your guns and following through. We have practiced and prepared for the moment, you have chosen your words, and you are focused on your body language.

Take a few deep breaths, count to five or ten if necessary, as this will prevent you from blurting out your assertion and coming across as aggressive. The added oxygen in your brain and your body is a natural way to increase your confidence, and it helps your posture.

Don't feel that you have to apologize. As we have seen, there are numerous assertive statements that you can choose from. It's about selecting one that feels natural to you. It may include a thank you or sorry, or it may not. That is up to you.

End the conversation or change the subject. It's not necessary that the conversation lasts more than a few minutes. The longer it lasts, the more likely the other person will be able to change your mind or use manipulative techniques. Walk away from any conversation that makes you uncomfortable and remember that it is not because you have done anything wrong. You have every right to stand up for yourself.

It's also important that you may not get it perfectly right the first time around. But this is not the same as doing something wrong. Every new skill needs to be practiced. You may find that sometimes you will feel like you are too passive or possibly a little aggressive for your own liking. It's all about finding a balance, and this is what we will work on next.

If you need some extra techniques to confidently stand up for yourself, here are a few more ideas you can put into action:

• Know what is bothering you. You might start blurting out things that may only make sense to yourself. On the contrary, you may retreat and say nothing, but people cannot guess what you are thinking; they will only assume. Understand what is bothering you and address this first.

• Don't allow others to tell you how you feel. Even your closest friends don't always know how you feel in a particular situation. Don't accept other people saying things like "You're just feeling tired because you stayed up too late." Only you know the reason why or if you are even tired.

• Think about the other person's perspective. You can still stand up for yourself and be empathetic toward other people. Trying to see things from different points of view will enable you to come up with an alternative that can solve many problems. It also helps with your emotional intelligence.

• Ride out the storm. This might sound as if we are going against the concept of standing up for ourselves, but it goes back to knowing which battles to fight. When someone verbally attacks you, you should stand up for yourself with the above techniques. But, if it's a person that has absolutely no respect for you, there is little point in engaging with them. Ride it out and either discuss the situation when they have calmed down or send an email/message.

• Respect the other person if you want to be respected in return. This means listening, not raising your voice, and appreciating boundaries. Though we will talk about this in more detail later, respect is crucial for healthy communication.

Don't leave unfinished business. This means that you haven't completely stood up for yourself until you have said everything you needed to say. Avoid walking away with the sensation that there is more to get off your chest. This type of thing can lead to the issue growing over time.

CHAPTER 10: BALANCE IS THE KEY

L earning the difference between passive and aggressive behavior is a tricky business. It is like walking a tightrope with each extreme on the end of the pole that is helping you to stay balanced. Just the tiniest gust of wind can knock you to the ground. On top of this, we frequently put too much pressure on ourselves to get it right, and this pressure makes it even harder to remain on the tightrope. You know how much harder it is to keep your balance when you look down? Well, the pressure we put on ourselves is like looking down; it rarely helps!

In this chapter, we will take a closer look at the characteristics and behaviors of aggressive and passive people. Being aware of both will allow us to assert ourselves but still be the kind person we are. This isn't about changing your personality in any way. Like assertiveness, passiveness and aggression are learned. People aren't born to be naturally aggressive. Life takes its toll, and we feel it is the only way we are able to communicate our message. It is true that certain personalities will adopt these characteristics more easily. People who are shy tend to be more passive. Too much confidence can appear as aggressive, depending on other factors like their body language.

Learning the Signs of Passive Behavior

Here is quite an extensive list of how a passive person will come across. While part of our learning is about making ourselves more assertive, it is also wise to look out for these characteristics in other people because it will help you with your communication.

A passive person may:

• Be afraid to speak up regarding their opinions or ideas

• Speak softly or quietly

• Avoid eye contact, often looking at the floor or focusing on other objects in the room

• Not show expression

• Slouch

• Withdraw or isolate themself from groups

• Agree with what people are saying, even if this goes against their feelings and beliefs

• See themself as having less value than those around them

• Be willing to cause themself suffering instead of others

• Ensure others are happy before themself

• Struggle to set or reach goals

Passive people fear assertion because they are worried that they won't be a nice person when doing so. Being passive is often associated with being too nice. In many situations, this fear stems from overstepping the balance, and they worry that they will come across as aggressive.

What Does an Aggressive Person Look Like?

Aggression can be physical or verbal. Verbal aggression isn't just shouting. It can also be the language we choose to use. For those on the receiving end, it is normal to fear verbal aggression becoming physical. Physical aggression, in the worst cases, can be an attack on a person's body from a gentle shove to hitting, and regardless of the extent, it is unacceptable.

Here are other signs of an aggressive person:

• They will interrupt a conversation or talk over other people

• Their voice will be loud. To a passive person, it may seem as if they are shouting

• Eye contact will be too long, staring, and often dominating

• Facial expressions can be intimidating

• Posture will be rigid, and their arms crossed in front of them

• They will invade the personal space of others

• They will try to control groups

• Their own feelings will be the only importance, shown by the demands they make of others

- In order to reach their goals, they may trample over others and hurt them

How Passive-Aggressive Behavior Can Harm Us

Passive-aggressive people are fully aware of their behavior, which is why in some cases, it can hurt more than aggression. Because of the cunning nature, it might be harder to spot passive-aggressive behavior, but here are some things to look out for:

- The person will criticize and protest

- They might be irritable

- They will purposely forget things

- They might perform tasks below standard

- They could be cynical

- A passive-aggressive person will complain when you make demands

- They will also complain that they are unappreciated

- They will be stubborn and unwilling to compromise

- It is normal for them to blame others when things don't go to plan

Dealing with the Three Behaviors

We have already talked about how to deal with passive-aggressive people. There should be no room for this in any of your relationships because it is an unhealthy form of communication. It is important that you make the person aware of their behavior. It might be worth keeping detailed notes of each act so that you can present them with the facts. Tell the person how you expect to be treated in clear, to the point statements. You may even consider reporting passive-aggressive behavior in the workplace to a superior, particularly when it is impacting the quality of your work.

Any form of physical aggression must be reported to the appropriate authority. This is not about being unkind or dramatic. If your partner is physically aggressive, this may be one of the hardest things you have to do, but you need to report it. The chances of it happening again are high, and you never know how bad it could get the next time.

People who are angry and start to shout or throw things are not in a state to see reason. Your efforts to calm them down will do little good, plus, it is not your responsibility. The aggressive person is the only person who is responsible for their behavior. Let them know that we will not tolerate this type of behavior and that you are happy to readdress the situation when they have calmed down.

We will take a look at more specific techniques to handle aggressive and passive-aggressive people in the next chapter.

I have always found the hardest people to deal with, ironically, are passive people. Both aggression and passive aggression can fit into a boundary that we know people can't cross. But there is so much empathy toward a fellow passive person that you don't want them to have to feel the same way you do.

It is important not to try and take control. You may seem like you are helping them, but you both need to discover your path to assertiveness. Find a comfortable surrounding where you will both be able to express how you feel. Ask questions about the other person's opinions and ideas and encourage them to ask you questions. Think about how you would like to be treated as an assertive person and treat them in the same way.

Finding Your Balance

Respect is the key! As long as you are polite and respectful, you can explore your behavior with other people until you find what you might call the sweet spot. You will know when you find it because you will start to see other people paying more attention to your words. You will feel the respect that they have for you, and you will feel like you are a valuable part of the group or conversation. At the same time, you will still feel like a kind person.

Look at some of the examples between the three types of responses that can be used in different situations.

A friend asks to borrow money:

- Passive – I guess so, how much do you need?

- Assertive – I have a policy not to lend money to friends.

- Aggressive – No way am I lending you money.

Your sister/brother shows up at your house unexpected:

- Passive – Oh, I didn't know you were coming.

- Assertive – I would have preferred it if you had called first.

- Aggressive – What are you doing here?

Your colleague tells you that you have to work overtime because they have plans:

• Passive – Well, I had plans, but okay.

• Assertive – Sorry, but that isn't going to work for me.

• Aggressive – I'm not doing all of your work again.

While you are learning to find your sweet spot, pay close attention to other people's communication. Identify things that other people do and say that you like. Decide if this is how you would like to be treated. If you witness things you are uncomfortable with or don't like, you know it's a type of behavior that you should avoid. For example, I watched a conversation where one person kept tapping the table with their pen. I felt this was aggressive as it seemed like the person didn't have the patience to listen to what was being said, and they wanted the other person to hurry up. I made a note to make sure this wasn't a behavior I adopted.

How to Be Assertive and Have Fun

For so long, the thought of being assertive would have terrified you, and in the early days, it may take a little while to begin to relax into your assertiveness. It won't be long before you actually start to enjoy it and to have more fun in your life. As your confidence begins to grow and you prioritize the things that you enjoy, life becomes fun. You are doing the things you want to do with the people you want. You have time to yourself and you can feel healthier.

There is absolutely no reason why you can't have fun and continue to be assertive. Telling a joke or retelling a funny story can still be done assertively without losing its humor. Sometimes people will constantly try and guess the punchline, and you need to gently remind them to be patient. Not everyone has the same type of humor, so don't worry if not everyone finds it funny. It's not a sign that they don't like you. Always make sure the joke or story is suitable for the audience and not on a topic that could cause offense.

You can look forward to more fun in your life. Being able to express how you really feel will let others learn more about you. Your relationships will become stronger and more meaningful. You will stop fearing the reactions of others. And all of these things mean that the events and activities that you participate in will be more fun than you imagined compared with just a short time ago when you were people pleasing.

There are still other behaviors that we need to learn how to handle. While the feelings and emotions of others are not something that you can control, there are things that can be done to help the situation.

CHAPTER 11: LEARNING HOW TO HANDLE THE VARIOUS TYPES OF TREATMENT FROM OTHERS

I f only we could assert ourselves knowing that the other person would simply say "Ok." Imagine how much easier life would be if we could say no to our boss and not fear being singled out in the future. Or to be able to tell our parents that we don't want to join them for Christmas and not feel more guilt than you can carry.

Unfortunately, this is not how life works, and we have to be prepared to handle every type of treatment that we may receive from saying no, from tears to insults.

Though I have said this on numerous occasions, it has to be reiterated as it is so important for the success of standing up for yourself.

Saying no or asserting your opinion is not a bad thing. You are in control of how you feel when you assert yourself. You have to accept that it is not only okay to assert yourself, but it is also good.

With the techniques we have practiced, you can learn to control your fear and guilt of saying no. But you cannot control the other person's feelings. While you can manage the situation by remaining calm yet assertive, you have to also accept that you can't control it. Healthy communication depends on both parties involved.

Let's break down possible ways people could treat us after we are assertive.

Coping with Aggression

Normally, when someone becomes aggressive, we take it personally, as if it was our fault that this person is now angry. They didn't like what they heard. The fact is that aggression often flares up when a person feels threatened. If you take your boss as an example, they might feel the pressure of your assertiveness because they've gotten used to getting their way with you and would now need to find someone else to do all of the things that you put up with doing. Your friends might feel threatened because they won't have the same control over you. Their aggression may come from fear, but they don't have the right communication skills to express this, and therefore, they get angry. We aren't making excuses for them, but it always helps to see the other person's point of view.

Understanding that the aggression is coming from feeling threatened helps you to be more focused on your actions, in particular, making sure that you don't unintentionally become more threatening.

1. Revise your body language. Make sure that you are open and that you maintain the right amount of eye contact so that the other person knows you aren't intimidated.

2. Avoid fast movements. Waving arms frantically doesn't create a sense of calm. Make an effort to respect a person's personal space.

3. Be polite, no matter what the other person does. It shows that you are respectful and not about to react to anger with anger.

4. Listen to what the other person is saying. Explain that you do understand and rather than discussing the negative comments, keep the attention on anything positive.

5. Don't say things like "You must calm down" or "You can't speak to me this way." Both are true, but you should stick to assertive "I" statements, such as "I don't like being shouted at in this manner."

6. Don't say yes just because they became angry. They will never learn to respect your assertiveness. Keep saying no in a calm, respectful manner until they accept it.

7. If they don't accept your no or your opinion, come back to the subject when they have calmed down.

8. Process your experience. Write about it in your journal or talk to someone about what happened. Understanding your feelings and working through them will reduce the likelihood of you replaying the situation in your head or losing sleep over it.

9. Don't tell yourself things like "They were just having a bad day." Everyone has bad days, but not everyone takes it out on others. You shouldn't have to make excuses for them.

10. Never underplay the impact the aggressive behavior has had on you. Whether it is personal or professional, if someone had overstepped a legal or ethical boundary, it should be reported.

The goal is to diffuse the situation, and this is going to take a degree of self-control. It's unlikely that you will attack back, but you also need enough self-control not to withdraw from the situation.

Handling Manipulation

No one is ever perfect, and most people can probably look back at a time when they have used manipulation to get what they want. The puppy eyes come out and the bottom lip drops for that last piece of chocolate. We can cope with this. We are talking about people who can spot your weaknesses and use them to their own advantage. The Parent-Teacher Association (PTA) knows that you won't say no to baking 200 cupcakes for the bake sale, and when you try to tell them that you don't have time, they reply with comments like "but nobody bakes cupcakes like you."

If you have just come back from your holidays and your boss asks you to work overtime, it would be manipulative for them to criticize you for saying no because you just had a lovely refreshing break. Misleading people, telling lies, and ignoring people are all forms of manipulation. They haven't liked what they heard, and they are using tactics to play on your vulnerabilities to get what they want. When your partner doesn't clean the floors properly, knowing that you will have to redo it, they are being passive-aggressive, which is still a form of manipulation. Manipulative people need a firmer hand.

1. Be more determined with your no. Don't feel the need to follow up with empathy or alternatives.

2. Manipulative people love to play the victim, and they want you to feel as if it is your fault. For this reason, don't apologize because it isn't you who needs to take responsibility for your behavior.

3. Let insults roll off you. The insults and criticism they throw at you is so that you will react. They want to see what buttons they can push. If you react in an emotional way, you become the dramatic one. Tell them that it is a shame they feel that way and walk away.

4. Have faith in your instincts. Manipulators can control by creating doubt. They want you to doubt a situation, feeling, or even yourself. Deep down you know what you want, and you have thought hard about your decision. Don't allow them to cause any form of doubt in yourself.

5. Ignore any pressure that is put on you. The fear of loss or the need for an answer straight away is unnecessary pressure. When a salesperson tells you the product won't be available later on, they are manipulating you into making a purchase straight away. There are few non-urgent things in life that require an immediate answer.

6. Don't try to change a manipulative person. You can express your dislike at the behavior and that you won't tolerate being treated in that way, but this won't change them. At best, we can stop them from treating you in this way.

I have so little time for people who are passive-aggressive or manipulative. They think that they are the smarter ones, but really, they are just lacking the ability to communicate in a healthy way. They lack emotional intelligence. Despite all of your best efforts, people may still try to manipulate you, and in this case, the best thing to do is keep your distance. There are plenty of amazing people who will treat you as you deserve to be treated. You don't need manipulators—even when they try to make you feel like you do!

What to Do When People Shame You for Being Assertive

When someone shames you for being assertive, it is not the same as what we spoke about earlier on in the book about shame and guilt. Guilt is the feeling you have when you do something bad, but shame is the feeling that you are bad.

Let's say you have stood up to a colleague and told them that you don't agree with their methodology. There is no reason to feel guilt or shame, as you have exercised your right to express your opinion in a kind, respectful way. If the colleague turns around and calls you a complete idiot in front of everyone, they have shamed you. You feel hurt, humiliated, and probably so shocked that you are unable to respond. Instead, you turn bright red and wish that the ground would swallow you whole.

Here is how you can handle people who shame you for asserting yourself.

1. Don't react. Your entire body, including your mouth and brain, might be in shock, which is a good thing. It prevents you from reacting before the brain kicks in. Without taking a moment to fully appreciate the whole situation, you run the risk of being humiliated more.

2. Don't apologize as you haven't done anything wrong. Saying sorry for something that isn't your fault can lead the bully to continue the attack.

3. Consider if the person's shaming was an unsuccessful attempt at constructive criticism. It's still not an excuse but it will help you communicate with them later.

4. When the situation (be that a family gathering, an event with friends, or a work meeting) is over, ask when a good time would be to speak to the person privately.

5. Let the person know that you are not happy with the way you were treated. That it is not necessary. "I do appreciate constructive feedback, but I don't appreciate being humiliated for voicing my opinion." It is likely that they didn't mean for you to take offense.

6. Let the person know that if they have a problem, you would like them to discuss it with you in private, rather than the whole group. If they have a problem with their communication skills, they can at least make sure that they talk to you individually and not in front of others. It will also make it

easier for you to find the confidence to assert yourself when it is just the two of you instead of a whole group.

7. Don't take any shaming personally and don't allow it to affect your self-esteem. You did everything the right way and should be proud of your progress. Focus on the positive to protect how you view yourself.

From experience, unless you are feeling particularly confident, you should react in the moment.

There is too much risk that the person will continue to belittle you, and it becomes harder to assert yourself. It may only undo the hard work you have done. That's not to say that the person should be left to get away with it.

Once again, it's about choosing the right time to assert yourself so that you are prepared and confident to handle the situation.

How to Cope with the Stress That Comes About from Asserting Yourself

Don't worry. This is a temporary stress while you are mastering your skills. The more you practice, the less anxiety and stress you will start to feel, and the process starts to become more natural. Until this moment arrives, there are some techniques for you to practice to lower the stress you feel when the time comes to being assertive.

Accept assertiveness as a challenge

Rather than looking at assertiveness as the cause of your stress, see it as a challenge or an obstacle that you need to overcome in order to become a stronger person. This challenge is going to help you become more emotionally resilient.

Accept the things that you cannot change

The impatient lady is going to skip the line in front of you and assume she did nothing wrong. The arrogant driver is going to steal the parking spot you were about to reverse into. None of this you can change.

These situations where people abuse their own position or take advantage of your kindness shouldn't be a cause for stress because it is a reflection of their behavior, not yours.

Chew gum

Okay, when I say chew gum, I don't mean with your mouth open so that everyone can hear each munch. That's enough to annoy anyone. Chewing gum promotes blood flow to your brain and causes brain waves similar to what a relaxed person experiences.

Laugh the stress away

Before you assert yourself, you will take time to prepare yourself and what you want to say. In between this and the conversation, watch a video online of something that will make you laugh. Laughing relieves your stress response and can help relax the tension in your muscles, which will also help with your body language.

Stop procrastinating

Do I say no, or don't I say no? You have already made the decision to assert yourself. Debating the decision further is likely to build up the stress. If this is the day before or even a few days, it will start to affect your health.

Take deep breaths

Aside from delivering more oxygen to your brain and body, deep breaths can help to slow your heart rate down and bring about a sense of peace and calm.

These practices are designed to help you in the moment so that you can reduce the build-up of stress before you need to say no or speak your mind.

The following techniques will help you reduce the stress you feel on a day-to-day basis.

• **Listen to music.** Soothing music can lower the blood pressure, the heart rate, and the stress hormones.

• **Enjoy nature.** Nature is a wonderful way to enjoy the moment and appreciate the beauty in the world and tranquility. Parks, woods, and forests allow you to take in the color green, which has a calming effect.

• **Practice yoga, meditation, and mindfulness.** All three are great ways to bring yourself back to the present, to relax your mind, and to remove negative thinking. As you replace negative thoughts with positive ones, you can literally feel the stress leave your body.

• **Exercise.** Exercising has many benefits. You will feel more confident in your body, you will be able to sleep better, and you can gain from the released endorphins.

- **Use essential oils.** Certain scents are known to be especially soothing and help you relax. Try lavender, roman chamomile, bergamot, or sandalwood.

- **Think about supplements.** Lemon balm, omega-3 fatty acids, green tea, and kava. Kava is used to help lower anxiety and stress. Double-check with your doctor if you have any other medical conditions.

Professional Treatment

In extreme cases, you might not be able to cope alone. This is normally when there are underlying issues that are restricting your ability to assert yourself, for example, abuse or trauma. Again, if you feel that you need professional help, please know that it doesn't mean that you have failed. You will still have learned an awful lot and made significant changes to your life. See it like you are so close to reaching the top shelf but you just need a boost.

Cognitive-behavioral therapy (CBT) is a type of therapy that involves talking. The theory behind CBT is that all of our thoughts, sensations, feelings, and actions are linked. CBT looks at untangling our interconnected problems so that each one is more manageable. It is often used to treat anxiety and depression, among other health problems.

Of all the things we have discussed in this chapter, there is probably one thing that we should focus on, and that is coping with stress. The reactions of other people are not a given. While it is good to prepare for all outcomes, we can't assume that this is how people are always going to react when we assert ourselves. These are extreme circumstances that you may never have to face. It is much more likely that the person will push a little and accept your second assertion, maybe even your first.

Stress, on the other hand, is something that we have to face on a regular basis, whether that is from standing up to for yourself or any of the other challenges we face in our lives. Learning how to cope with stress will help us to enhance our overall well-being. When we are feeling more positive about life in general, it is easier to face the difficulties, and that includes conflict resolution, which we will explore in the next chapter.

CHAPTER 12: CONFLICT RESOLUTION

L ooking at the bigger picture, isn't it just incredible that there aren't more conflicts in our lives? One a day may seem like a lot, but let's consider the potential risks for conflict.

Imagine all of the religions and spiritual beliefs in the world that can encourage strong opinions, not to mention political views. Cultures and languages are fascinating but can also lead to miscommunications. The pressure of our relationships can sometimes cause us to break, maybe over something apparently insignificant or it arises from larger underlying issues. Your toddler throws a tantrum because you won't let them eat dog food, or your teenager disagrees with absolutely everything because life is just so unfair.

I once went to a dinner party that had guests who spoke English and Spanish. You could sense that there was a little tension in the air, but only because it wasn't always easy to be understood. As people started to relax, the conversation began to flow. That was when we discovered that we had a retired bullfighter and a vegetarian who sat next to each other. The potential for disaster was huge.

Because we are all so different, it is common to expect some degree of conflict in our lives. To avoid it would mean pretty much staying at home by yourself for days and weeks at a time. We shouldn't shy away from conflict but instead, learn how to resolve it so that it can become a part of our healthy relationships.

Key Considerations Regarding Conflict

Conflicts arise when people are at odds. It could be because of disagreements in values, needs, perceptions, ideas, dreams, or goals.

● It is more complex than a disagreement. Either person or even both will feel like there is a threat, regardless of whether the threat is real.

● Our response to a conflict will depend on our perceptions, which have been influenced by our life experiences, as well as our values and culture.

● Conflicts create strong emotions, and it is essential that we are able to control our emotions in order to resolve conflicts.

● Resolving conflicts in a healthy way allows all types of relationships to flourish, as both people can feel more secure and trust is strengthened.

Like many difficult situations, ignoring conflicts or brushing them under the rug will not mean that the issue has been resolved. On the contrary, our feelings tend to intensify. This is because the perceived threat is still present even when we bottle up our emotions. Until this threat is addressed, the conflict won't be resolved.

People pleasers and others who struggle to assert themselves will avoid conflict, disagreements, and arguments at all costs. If we can learn how to handle conflicts correctly, there will be fewer arguments. Instead of seeing conflict as a bad thing, we should look at it as another opportunity to learn and grow.

Let's begin by looking at examples of unhealthy responses to conflict:

• A person may struggle to see what matters to other people or respond to their needs.

• They might express negative emotions such as anger and frustration in explosive bursts.

• The other person might feel abandoned as love is held back.

• There may be no room for compromise.

• Avoiding the conflict because they assume that the outcome will be a bad one.

Not being able to resolve conflict in a healthy manner can lead to upset feelings and disappointment, and if it continues, it may be impossible to reverse the situation. In personal relationships, it might result in the division of families. In professional relationships, not only does the atmosphere become difficult to work in for everyone, but it can also affect the quality of the project or product.

How you handle conflict will depend on two essential skills: stress relief and emotional awareness.

The Importance of Stress Relief in Conflict Management

To resolve conflict successfully, you are going to have to be able to relieve stress quickly. It is often our stress that pulls our attention away and causes us to lose focus. Like passiveness and aggression, there is a necessary balance that is required when managing stress.

• Too much stress and your stress response will be one of anger, built-up emotion, and an inability to keep still.

• Not enough stress and you will find yourself lacking the energy to handle the conflict. It is easier to withdraw and become depressed.

• Your stress may also cause you to freeze from the tension or the pressure.

Either of the stress responses above will mean that we are unable to clearly receive the other person's message. The verbal communication and body language can't be clearly understood. It will also be a challenge to recognize your own feelings and communicate these feelings or needs clearly. Stress is like a dam that blocks the flow of a river, with the water being our communication.

Because of the amount of pressure we feel in our lives, it might actually be difficult to know what stress feels like. It has become so common that we seem to learn to live with it, like the niggly ache in your body. Symptoms may vary from person to person but can include anxiety, depression, difficulty in concentrating, irritability, and low self-esteem. Physical symptoms may present as low energy, headaches, stomachache, insomnia, low sex drive, and a weak immune system.

Since I've gone into great detail with stress management techniques in the previous chapter, I won't repeat everything again here. However, remember that there are techniques to help you in the moment of conflict like deep breathing and laughing. There are also invaluable techniques that will help you manage your stress over the long-term, such as exercise, yoga, and meditation.

The Role of Emotional Awareness in Conflict Resolution

Emotional awareness is the ability to recognize one's own feelings and the feelings of others. It's a simple concept, but one we tend not to practice. If something or someone makes us sad, we don't have time to examine the extent of the sadness or if there are other emotions behind it. We might be sad because we have lost someone or sad because someone has embarrassed us. More often than not, you can recognize that you feel sad but put it to one side and continue with life.

For successful conflict resolution, it is necessary to pay attention to your emotions as they arise. To let yourself feel them and be aware of their effects on how you view a situation.

Being aware of emotions will enable you to understand more about the following:

- What is actually bothering you?

- What is actually bothering others?

- Remain motivated to fully resolve the conflict

- Enhance your communication

- Reduce the tension in a conflict

Here are some questions you can ask yourself so that you are more aware of your emotions.

1. Do your emotions change along with your experiences?

2. Do you have any physical symptoms that appear with certain emotions, for example, a sickness in your stomach or a nervous twitch?

3. Are others aware of your emotions based on your body language? Perhaps a raised eyebrow when you are displeased?

4. Are you able to experience extreme emotions? Rather than anger, can you feel infuriated?

5. Do your emotions gain the attention of others?

6. Do your emotions play a role in your decision making?

These questions aren't designed to make you feel bad or paranoid about your feelings. The answer may not be a simple yes or no. You may not be able to answer the questions. It is a good idea to spend some time thinking about these questions while you are with friends and loved ones, at work, or even when you are exercising. Gain a better understanding of how various circumstances impact your feelings. Educating yourself in this way will make it easier to resolve conflicts as they come up.

How to Resolve Conflicts with Confidence and Assertion

Excellent communication is the first step to resolving conflict. This includes the words you choose and the way you say them. Telling someone that you understand their point of view when your arms and legs are crossed is giving mixed signals since your body is contradicting what your words are saying. Being able to fully listen to what is being said and not interrupting the other person will also be incredibly productive.

Let's look at other methods to resolve conflict.

Let go of the need to win

So many times a conflict escalates because of the need to win the battle or to be right. This shows an unwillingness to see things from alternative perspectives and that there is no room for give and take. You may be right, you may be wrong, but it shouldn't be what matters. Resolution is the goal, not winning.

Don't bring past resolutions into the current conflict

Once you have learned how to resolve conflicts, this won't be an issue because each one will be dealt with so that you can put it in the past. If there are still things that upset you about moments from the past, now isn't the time to bring them up. Doing so just becomes a negative trip down memory lane. And it is often not relevant to the issue at present.

Consider if the conflict is worth it

Not everything has to be a battle. Sometimes it's just not worth the energy that conflict can take away from you. Maybe the waiter was rude, but if you aren't planning on going back to that restaurant, do you need to point this out to them? If it is something that you won't be able to let go of, then definitely discuss how you feel.

Learn how to forgive

The point of conflict resolution is to get everything out on the table so that it doesn't continue to eat away at you. If you can't forgive someone, it means that the conflict hasn't been resolved, and it will reappear later down the road.

Using humor to resolve conflict

Needless to say, there is a right way and a wrong way, the right time and a wrong time to use humor, but there is a very good reason why humor is the best medicine. In a tense situation, one person with a witty comment can have the whole room laughing. The heavy atmosphere is instantly lifted, and it becomes easier to resolve the conflict as people are more relaxed.

In relationships, humor can bring a couple closer together, especially if you have an inside joke that the two of you share. Humor also allows you to put the situation in perspective, often seeing that the problem isn't as big as it may have originally seemed. If there is a battle to win the conflict, humor can often break this power struggle, so you are both back on an even playing field.

When using humor to resolve conflicts, bear in mind the following points:

- You both need to be in on the joke. It can't be a one-sided attempt at humor that the other person may find insulting or offensive.

- The humor has to make you both laugh together. If only you find it funny, then really you are only laughing at the other person.

- Your humor can't cover up emotions. You can't find something funny when you are only laughing to hide your disappointment. You will take the disappointment with you while the other person is under the impression that the conflict is resolved.

- It has to be funny! Not everyone is naturally funny. We may have to learn a few jokes or watch a few comedy series to pick up some ideas. Don't be afraid to make a joke of yourself while you are still learning how to be funny.

- Be very careful of sarcasm. Some people are able to pull it off, but for many others, sarcasm is just the lowest form of wit. Sarcasm can hurt people's feelings. When it is in the form of verbal irony, it can be quite amusing but requires a level of intelligence, common sense, and wit.

I find a few comforting similarities between assertiveness and conflict resolution. We fear both, but this fear is unjustified. We often think that both are bad things and that they are impossible to master. In reality, like assertiveness, conflict resolution is a skill that needs to be learned and practiced. It requires an understanding of yourself as well as those around you and a focus on your words and actions. Rather than seeing conflict resolution as something negative, we must learn to see it for what it is; a way to strengthen our relationships so that we can reduce our stress and enjoy the time we spend with people, and essentially, our lives.

CHAPTER 13: ASSERTIVENESS IN THE REAL WORLD

While coaching clients and from my own experience, I have learned that reading the advice and techniques provided only takes a person so far.

It is sometimes necessary to work through some real-life examples to see the theory in practice.

It's like wanting to know how a bread machine works; you have your recipe, but you want to try one out before you buy a machine for yourself.

So far, I have provided you with the ingredients and the instructions.

This chapter is going to test a bread making machine and see how everything fits together to get the desired results.

Then, you will feel more confident about buying your own bread machine – or being assertive!

A driver cuts in front of you

This is a perfect example of learning when to let a situation go — a battle that is not worth fighting. There are too many stories of people asserting themselves and it becomes dangerous.

Even if someone dangerously cuts in front of you and you instinctively reach for the horn, you may find that you've angered the other driver.

There have been cases on the news where road rage has led to an angry driver blocking the other car, getting out, and physically attacking the innocent driver. It's not worth it!

Talk to a friend or relative about how you felt so that you can process your feelings and put them behind you.

Phone salespeople

Even a people pleasing non-assertive person can get irritated by the persistence of a phone salesperson.

Firstly, it's a huge invasion of your privacy and your time. The good thing is that there is a distance between you, so you don't have to fear any physical repercussions. It is also very unlikely that they will become angry with you.

The problem is their persistence. Understand that these people probably work on commission, so their persistence is related to their income. Also, be aware that they have been trained in techniques to turn your no into a yes.

Politely thank them for their time and say no, you are not interested. The second no will have to be firmer, but if you say it with a smile, you will still sound friendly. The third no can include empathy, such as "I understand you are doing your job, but this is the third time I am saying no. Have a good day." Worst case scenario you may have to hang up.

Your children don't respect your authority

There is often less fear associated with assertiveness and your children, but there are many more emotions. Parents fear they are doing a bad job, or that the situation will only get worse as they get older.

The great thing now is that you can teach your children how to be assertive, so they don't have the same problems as you did. The first problem with children ignoring your authority is that they have little respect for you. This works both ways, so you both have to learn how to show each other more respect.

It is essential that you communicate in a clear and calm manner, no electronic devices to distract them. Asserting yourself with your children requires consistency in your words and actions.

One example was a mum who was fed up with cleaning her daughter's bedroom.

She had asked so many times, but nothing had been done. She told her daughter that if she didn't clean her room, she would take a plastic bag and everything on the floor would go in the bin, and that was exactly what happened.

Children won't respect authority if they are used to empty threats and promises.

Your boss has unpredictable mood swings

One day your boss is patting you on the back and one of your best friends, and the next they are screaming at you for a mistake you didn't make. It's incredibly difficult to gauge the reaction you are going to get each time.

In this situation, you need to take your focus off the boss and place it on your job and the task at hand.

Bosses who have a nasty temper and fly off the handle don't really care about the well-being of their team, and to protect your mental health, it is worth taking on just a hint of the same mentality.

You should feel that you are equal. While they are your boss, you are both human beings and deserve the same fair treatment.

If your boss happens to get angry or start shouting, remain tall and maintain your eye contact. Don't let them intimidate you. Listen carefully, there may be some further instructions or things that you could do to improve the job—not yourself! Smile, say thank you or okay, and keep going.

Once you have considered your boss's words, recognized how you feel and prepared yourself, you can ask to talk to them one-on-one. Use "I" statements to tell them how you feel.

Be careful of the word humiliated; a manipulative boss will use this to their advantage. "I feel disrespected when you shout." A personal favorite is "I don't understand what you are trying to say when you shout." You have successfully asserted yourself but also educated them on their communication skills.

You are a teacher and need to exert your authority

I was very pleased with my assertive progress, but one day when I went into a school to talk to a group of teenagers, I seriously doubted my ability to assert myself. It was terrifying.

Kids are so smart, they can read us like a book. Within seconds they have summed up exactly what is going on and what they can get away with. Teachers, like parents, need to be consistent with their behavior and they need to be fair. Classroom expectations need to be clearly outlined and explained. This is like setting boundaries that students know they can't cross.

It is likely you will have to discipline students at some point but do so privately. It's more respectful, and there is no reason for the whole class to see. Plus it disrupts the flow of the lesson and causes distractions. Don't be scared to use a little humor to resolve conflicts and help clear some of the tension in the air.

You are on the verge of burnout at work

When you spend weeks, months, and even years trying to please everyone at work, it is going to take its toll on both your professional and personal life.

There might be various people in the office that you need to be more assertive with. Start with those you have a more friendly relationship with as it will boost your confidence. When someone asks you to do something, tell them that you can't, but you will talk about it with them tomorrow once you have looked at your timetable. Make a decision whether it is possible and think of solutions that may suit you both. If your decision is no, tell them with a positive attitude that you can't without explaining your reasoning. If they insist, you can tell them that your agenda is full.

Don't let the other person start trying to rearrange your agenda, as that would be crossing a boundary. If the idea really terrifies you, send an email, but remember to keep it as equally short as a face-to-face conversation.

A salesperson has embarrassed you

When a saleswoman giggled at the size of my ex-girlfriend's large feet and told her that she would have to go to the shop that sells extra-large sizes, my girlfriend smiled back and said, "I hope you don't speak to overweight people in the same way," walked out of the shop. I watched the saleswoman turn bright red.

My ex was polite. She didn't shout and she kept her anger under control. After a salesperson treats you badly, the chances are you will never go there again. Whether this person likes you or not shouldn't enter your mind. This could be a battle you chose not to fight, but I would use it as a way to practice asserting yourself on someone you won't ever see again.

A colleague keeps telling sexist jokes in front of you

This is a clear violation of your boundaries, not only your own boundaries but also the code of conduct in the workplace.

There are two lines of approach. First, you should let this person know that you don't find this type of humor very funny and that it is disrespectful to the opposite sex. They might listen to you, or they may enjoy the reaction and continue.

If they ignore you, it is time to report them to management, which can be done either verbally, or if you feel more comfortable, in writing.

Your partner interrupts you

The funny thing about people who interrupt is that the person often doesn't realize they are doing it. The not so funny thing is that interrupting is a form of domination and exerting power.

First, point out their behavior. Ask them why they keep interrupting. Making your partner aware of their bad habit may be enough for them to pay closer attention to it. Make sure your question doesn't sound rhetorical or as a statement.

If the interruptions keep coming, wait until they finish and ask if you can finish what you were saying. Every time, repeat the same words "Can I finish?" You might need to firmly tell them that your opinions and ideas are equally as important, and you deserve the opportunity to finish your sentences.

Your partner has come dangerously close to physical abuse

It's that situation when you are 99% convinced that they won't hit you, but there is still 1% of doubt. This doubt is enough to make you freeze in fear.

Stay frozen! Any words or actions may fuel the fire. Take a few seconds to catch your breath, centralize your thoughts. Give them the opportunity to do the same. Depending on the atmosphere, you might want to grab your keys and just get out so you can both have some space.

But it is essential that you sit down and talk about what happened. You need to be calm, so in the time that you are taking some space, do something that makes you happy, shout, scream, cry, go shopping, go to the gym, or the countryside.

Spend some time on self-love and fill yourself with deserving thoughts. You are a good person, you should be treated equally, and you have the right to feel safe in your relationship. Be very direct with your partner and let them know that you will not tolerate fear in a relationship.

If your partner immediately realizes that they have crossed the line, you may be able to have the conversation straight away.

While they may apologize, be careful of saying, "It's ok," because it is not okay, and you can't excuse them. You can tell them that you forgive them so that you are both able to move forward. Use this opportunity to talk to each other about what made the situation get out of hand.

Don't blame each other, so remember the "I" statements. You should never feel threatened in a relationship, but you can use this as a chance to communicate better and become stronger.

Your supervisor has put you on the spot

It's another one of those incidents when you may just freeze as you can't find the right words to say. Other people can't stop talking as they try to find the right words. Many of us just say yes.

The magic words here are "I will get back to you." By yourself, take the time to compose yourself. You can add a timeframe, like in five minutes or an hour, however long seems appropriate. Don't feel pressured into a no or a yes on the spot. In five minutes you might feel able to say yes, but you need time to decide if you are able and willing.

You need to overcome your fear of public speaking

It's a very common fear, so don't feel alone on this. Consider what is making you afraid of speaking in public. If you are worried you are going to make a mistake, practice, practice, and practice again.

If you are worried about what people are going to think of your speech, practice again in front of a friend and/or a relative. Get some feedback from then and make any changes you think will improve.

If you are worried about speaking in front of new people, do a little research on your audience.

Learning more about them will help you realize that they are just people, and it will help you feel like you aren't talking to strangers.

Your parents criticize your life choices

It's hard not to take this personally. If your parents don't agree with your choice of career or partner, you might start to doubt your own decisions.

Follow your instincts and decide if you are happy. If you put your hand on your heart and say you are happy, then it is time to tell your parents this.

Remind them that you are an adult and although you value their opinions, you have made your decision. They might take some time to come around, so make sure you provide opportunities for them to see your happiness.

Invite them over for dinner and tell them the great parts of your job. Avoid complaining because this will give them the chance to say, "I told you so."

Your feelings get all muddled and you can't express yourself

Sometimes, it's not the fear of asserting yourself but it's the confusion you feel in the process. Your emotions are wheezing around like a washing machine on full spin, and it is difficult to think straight, and even more difficult to get the right words out. It could be that you feel the need to say more than you need to, which is complicating things.

Slow down for a second, take a few deep breaths and stick to the shortest of assertive statements: "No, thank you," "I can't," "I don't like your behavior." Once you have got the first assertive statement done, you will have a reaction from the other person.

It's often saying that first statement that lets your brain start to calm down and you can see things more clearly.

Your friend won't accept that you don't want to go to a social event

Friends will use the typical sentences to try and persuade you "You know you will enjoy yourself when you get there" or "You need to get out more." Both might be true, but it doesn't mean to say you need to accept. If you don't want to go, stand your ground.

Don't tell them you have plans if you don't, you run the risk of them asking what you have planned and then having to lie. Statements like "Thanks for the invite, maybe next time" is enough. If they insist or ask for an explanation, you can tell them that you don't want to or that you aren't in the mood.

For the really insistent friends, "because I said no" is all the explanation you should feel you have to give. Use the broken-record technique if they don't stop. Do so in a positive way with a smile and even a hug when they accept your assertiveness. It will prevent them from feeling bad and feel that they can't invite you next time.

You are struggling to find a way to end a relationship

The difficulty you might find here is that you probably will have to provide an explanation, especially for long-term relationships. The other issue is that emotions are going to be very raw with both parties suffering.

It is essential to stay away from cliches, "It's not you, it's me," as this doesn't offer an explanation. Knowing why you want to separate and being able to explain this to the other person isn't the same. Think hard about the words you choose and ensure they clearly highlight the issues in the relationship.

It might not be enough to just say you aren't happy. The other person will want to know why. Listen to what the other person says and make sure you are answering their questions. Don't get defensive and start to blame them for your decision. Take responsibility for your mistakes in the relationship but don't rehash the issues over and over again. Breaking up with someone is never going to be easy, but being clear about your feelings using "I" statements will help communication.

Remember, being assertive during a breakup is actually fairer on the other person. They will be able to see that the relationship is definitely over and not cling on to the hope of getting back together.

Your child's teacher has insulted your parenting style

There are so many different ways you can educate children. Not everyone is going to agree on the same style. Teachers should be more than aware of this, but it is possible that one will strongly disagree.

In the first place, there is no need for insults. Secondly, research evidence that backs your choices. This will help you feel confident about your methods. Tell the teacher that you don't appreciate being insulted just because you raise your children in a certain way. Then tell them what you would appreciate.

Assertive communication is essential. You don't want to retaliate with insults or aggressive behavior because they may start to take this out on your child. Use the sandwich method by placing your assertive statement between two positive comments.

Your colleague keeps palming work onto you, telling you that you do it far better

This is a manipulative technique. You may have welcomed the compliment the first time, but now it is starting to get old.

The next time your colleague tries to give you extra work, pass it straight back to them with a smile and say, "Not today, thank you." Showing them that you have caught on to their tricks is often enough to make them move on to some other unfortunate person.

Avoid telling them that you don't have time. Though this is probably true, it's not about the time. It's about the fact that they are expecting you to work harder, so they don't have to.

Your friend is narcissistic

Narcissistic people feel that they are generally better than others. They think they are better looking, and this can lower your self-esteem.

They will assume their needs are more important than yours, and you will find that you always do what they want to do rather than what you want to do.

While it is not a healthy relationship, it doesn't mean that they are necessarily a bad person. It comes across as if they have an extremely high opinion of themselves but is likely to be the opposite and that their need for power comes from insecurity.

Start focusing on taking time to do the things you want to do, even if it means doing it without them.

When asserting yourself, use statements that start with "I need" to highlight that your needs also matter. Also, phrases like "I have other priorities" will show a narcissistic friend that they don't always come first.

Your mom/sister/aunt turns on the waterworks when you say no

Some people are naturally more emotional than others, and the slightest upset will have them in tears. Others have the ability to start crying just to make you feel bad.

First, figure out if your family member is purposely turning on the tears in order to get their way. If you feel this is the case, it is a form of manipulation, and you must be firm.

Make sure they are aware that you won't tolerate emotional games, and say, "I won't be pressured into making a decision" or "I'm not going to say yes just because you are upset." It sounds harsh, but it's not fair and can play on your weakness when they should be supporting you.

If you think that they are genuinely upset, ask them why they are upset. By understanding their feelings better, you will be able to suggest alternatives that you are willing to do that allows you the free time you need and stops them from feeling upset.

The physical symptoms are too much for you to handle

If your heart starts to race, your legs are shaking, and you feel the sweat dripping from your forehead because of the fear of the consequences, you are in no state to handle the conflict.

It is crucial that you smile, tell the person something simple like "I will get back to you" and walk away to regain a sense of calm. Concentrate on your breathing, inhale for ten, and exhale for another ten seconds. Once you start to feel your body calm down, you will be able to think better about the situation and plan what you want to say.

These are just a few situations where you can use the assertive techniques in this book to reach the desired outcome. It might be a toxic partner rather than a toxic boss, or a girlfriend that cries every time you try to assert yourself.

In the cases that you decide to assert yourself, always take a moment to understand your feelings as well as the other person's. Think about what you want to say and avoid procrastinating.

All assertive behavior is good and will bring about positive results when communication is healthy, open, and honest.

CHAPTER 14: THE IMPORTANCE OF ASSERTIVENESS AND RESPECT

Respect plays such an important role in assertiveness as well as in our relationships in general. It allows you to feel safe while being able to accept other people for who they truly are. Like assertiveness, respect doesn't come naturally, and it is something that is learned.

Let's take a look at what a respectful relationship looks like for both parties:

- You can freely express who you are and feel safe doing so

- You can discuss what you need and want

- When you disagree, you listen to what the other person says

- You don't shout or interrupt each other

- You don't try to control each other

- You take responsibility for your actions and your mistakes

• You appreciate the boundaries and space of each other

Others will define respect as admiration for someone's abilities, knowledge, or achievements. Respect also includes the regard of the rights and traditions of others. The ability to respect others can allow you to gain perspective, improve your lifestyle, and create meaningful relationships that encourage positive communication.

Without respect, it is common to see conflict in our relationships, and those people who need to be more assertive will struggle even more. If someone doesn't respect us, it will feel like any attempt to stand up for yourself will be met with anger or simply falling on deaf ears.

At the same time as respecting others, it is also necessary to learn how to respect yourself. With self-respect, you will find it easier to take risks that enable us to improve our confidence. When opportunities arise, self-respect will let you take them without fearing or doubting your abilities. To respect yourself, you need to take pride in yourself and to appreciate your worth. This is one of the keys to stopping people from treating you unfairly. One clear example of self-respect is being able to assert yourself so that you get what you deserve.

What Do We Deserve in Life?

It's a loaded question. There are certain things that we all deserve along with a number of things we may think we deserve. Everyone deserves the right to their own beliefs, cultures, and traditions. Everyone has the right to feel safe in their relationships, their jobs, and in life in general. Everyone deserves love, happiness, and respect. We also deserve to have time and space to discover all the things we want to do and experience in life.

When it comes to what we think we deserve, it becomes a little trickier. We might receive a type of love that you think you deserve, but you don't. Say, for example, you choose your family over your partner in certain situations. This doesn't mean you don't deserve complete love from your partner, or vice versa.

Some people feel that the world owes them a living and that each pay increase and promotion should just be given to them. Others put in the effort, as they really do deserve it, but it gets passed on to someone less deserving.

The lesson here is that what you deserve in life isn't the same as what you believe you deserve. Often settling for what you think you deserve will lead to unhappiness. If you don't think you deserve to be respected, you never will be.

How to Earn More Respect from Others

Respect is most definitely a two-way street. If you don't show respect, you won't receive any in return.

So, the first step is to start respecting others. This involves learning to listen to what people are saying, to appreciate differences and even ask questions so that you can learn more. You can also nurture a safe environment where people around you are able to express their feelings without fear of repercussions.

Here are some other ways to help you earn respect:

Be a nice person

It sounds obvious but it is easily overlooked. Have you noticed how the basics of being nice are slowly becoming a thing of the past? While culture still has an impact, there are still fewer "please" and "thank yous" in the world. Fewer people smile for no reason other than to be kind. Being nice doesn't cost us anything, perhaps a bit more effort when we are having a bad day, but it will encourage others to respect our kindness.

Be helpful

Now, we have to be very careful here because one of our biggest problems is being too helpful. Whenever someone asks us to do something to help them, we say yes. However, being asked to help and spotting the opportunity to assist without being asked is not the same. Learning to assert ourselves and say no doesn't mean that we still can't help those who are in need of it.

Don't allow yourself to make excuses

There might be genuine reasons for being late or not getting the project finished on time. There is little point in trying to make excuses or blame someone else. You will earn more respect if you can own up to any mistake, apologize, and make an effort for it not to happen again. See your mistakes as a chance to learn.

Free yourself from anger

Not letting go of anger has terrible consequences. It builds up inside of us, can affect our overall mood, and can lead to stress, depression, and other negative health issues. On the other hand, holding on to that grudge won't earn you any respect from those around you. It is healthier on all levels to learn how to let go of this anger so that you can move on.

Look for ways to become a better person

When we reach adulthood, it's easy to stop learning, or at least actively learning. We either become too busy or feel that we learn enough through our work. The truth is that continuous learning isn't about becoming smarter. It's about exploring more opportunities in the world, learning more about yourself, and building your confidence. You may think you have the job that you deserve because you don't possess other skills. But what if you took a course in website development or cooking and discovered that you have a whole new potential career that you love. The ability to change to the circumstances we face is something that deserves respect.

Keep your promises

When you make a promise, you are making a commitment. It's almost impossible to respect someone who makes a promise and then doesn't keep it. It's hard to respect someone who makes a promise that they never wanted to do in the first place.

Be open-minded until it goes against your morals

Whether you love someone or hate them, there is a great amount of respect for someone who refuses to go against their morals or their principles. Let's say a politician rubs you up the wrong way, but you can still respect them when they create an absolute anti-racism policy. Your morals and boundaries are there for a very good reason, and there shouldn't be room for negotiation. On the other hand, everything else, especially those things that we don't know enough about, should be met with an open mind.

Defend others

Even for non-assertive people, it is easier to defend others than it is yourself. If you see someone being mistreated, be there. It might be enough to offer a sympathetic ear, or you might need to point out the mistreatment. Use the skills we learned regarding conflict to point out any injustices.

Ignore your negative self-talk

Negative self-talk serves for one purpose and one purpose only- to bring us down. Negative self-talk is all of those little thoughts and ideas that creep up about yourself that make you feel incompetent or undeserving. It's the little voice that tells you that you can't do something or that you aren't capable of reaching your goals. Each time a negative thought comes up about yourself, instantly replace it with a positive one so that you learn how to respect yourself.

I do feel that a lot of what is required to be respectful is common sense, and we can probably still hear parents, grand-parents, or teachers reminding us of these behaviors. For one reason or another, some people haven't learned how to be respectful and other characteristics dominate more. This is particularly the case with narcissism, where the person has a me-first attitude. Be aware that despite your efforts, not everyone is capable of being respectful. This is not on you. We have already said that you are the only person who can control your feelings and your actions. If there are people who, no matter what you do, will still not respect you, you're better off creating some distance between you and this person.

How to Get What You Deserve in Life

So, in the first place, you have to be clear about what you want, and you have to be able to defend your opinion. Imagine James is at work, and he wants the promotion that two others want. Both of the other people are confident and assertive. Ask yourself why you should be the person to get the promotion. Write a list of why you deserve what you want. You are probably going to feel anxious about the idea of asserting yourself to get what you want, so preparation is key.

Once you have created your list, it's time to word your sentences so that they are short yet effective. The longer you make it, the more easily it becomes to get flustered or muddled. Your message must be clear.

Use "I" statements. "I have been working hard" or "I completed X and Y." Highlight your achievements in a positive way. If you are asserting yourself to get what you deserve in a relationship, you still need to use "I" statements. "I have been patient" or "I also have dreams."

Don't feel the need to put down other people who are in the race to get what you deserve. It doesn't do your case any favors, but it does start to feel like the school playground and tit for tat.

Before you have your assertive conversation to get what you deserve, practice your relaxation techniques, get a good night's sleep, and make sure you wake up in the best possible mood.

With the following six tips, you will be able to confidently ask for what you deserve in an assertive yet respectful manner.

1. What you ask for must be reasonable. There are a number of sales techniques that some might encourage you to use, asking for more than what you want in case the person offers less, starting with small requests and building your way up, etc. Maybe it's just easier to be honest and ask for what you want and deserve.

2. Find one reason for your request. It is good to prepare several in case the person doesn't accept your first reason, but with your initial request, only give one.

3. Consider other people's needs. While striving for what you want, how are others going to feel? You shouldn't be experiencing guilt because you have put your desires first. But if you deserve more commitment in a relationship, how will this make your partner feel?

4. The other person, whether it's your boss or your partner should have the opportunity to say no. You have the right to assert yourself and defend your position, but the other person also has the right to say no. This is the whole point of having a healthy, respectful relationship.

5. If someone says no, get over it. You can't sulk about it or take it personally. It's true it is hard, but there will be more

opportunities. It will be much better for your relationship if you can put it behind you with no resentment.

6. If you don't succeed in getting what you deserve the first time, don't give up. We don't always get what we deserve, but by asking, we may get at least what we need. If you never ask, you will never get what you deserve. Remember the saying, "It's better to be a lion for a day than a sheep for your whole life."

So, how does creating a respectful environment help you to be more assertive and get what you deserve? Really, it's like doing a lot of the foundation work prior to asserting yourself. With respect, you already have the right environment to communicate in a healthy way where you feel safe and don't fear the other person's reactions. Boundaries are already in place, and you have mastered the art of listening. Because of this close relationship, when you are respectful, you will discover that asserting yourself becomes more natural, and even the need becomes less frequent.

Finally, think of respect in this way: when you are aggressive, you are only respecting your own wishes; when you are passive, your respect for others is too much. Assertiveness is the right amount of respect for both others and yourself.

CHAPTER 15: HOW TO HELP YOUR LOVED ONES ASSERT THEMSELVES

S o far, we have looked at the assertiveness from the person who needs to make positive changes in their life. It has been us who have needed to work on our communication skills and gain more confidence. But what if you want to help someone else stand up for themselves? This chapter will be dedicated to the viewpoint of those watching a loved one struggle to assert themselves.

As assertion is such a vital skill, we are also going to spend some time on teaching children how to be assertive. This essential skill can help children to communicate with their peers better, understand more about their feelings, and reduce negative behavior in schools such as bullying.

Watching someone you love get pushed around and hurt by others can be heartbreaking. Before you jump in and try and rescue them, you need to take a moment to consider things from their point of view. Are they aware that they have a problem, or do they still see themselves as being a nice person? Are they ready to make a change? If they aren't aware of the problem, you will have to start with a conversation explaining your genuine concern for their well-being without telling them what they need to do.

People pleasers are constantly controlled by others. If you approach things the wrong way, you may become another person who is just telling them what to do rather than helping them.

Let's say your friend is under too much pressure at work, and on top of that, they have a pushy sister who is always asking for help looking after her kids. This person never has time to do things with you, but you know that deep down they want to. Although you completely understand that your friend doesn't have time, if you aren't careful about how you talk to your friend about their assertiveness, they might start feeling like you are putting more pressure on them.

Supporting Your Loved One While They Learn Assertive Skills

The people in your life who need to assert themselves more need love, praise, and to feel respected. They need someone they can talk to without feeling like they are being judged. They need a rock that they can lean on as they work through the process of learning and asserting. They don't need to be told that they are a doormat and that everyone is walking over them. This will cause them to feel worse about themselves. After all, they are just trying to be nice, and now they are being insulted for it.

Encourage the person to talk about their feelings. Ask them how they feel when they have too much on their plate. Find out what they think about saying no to others. Ask them about their goals and their hobbies. Never assume you know because circumstances change. Build a solid foundation where the person knows that you are there to help them when they want it.

Listen to them, listen eagerly as if everything they say matters. Never interrupt them, especially when they are unraveling their emotions. It will really help your loved one if they know that their words, ideas, and thoughts have value.

Find new activities that you can try together, making sure you ask their opinions about different ideas. The hope with this is that they find new interests that will encourage them to say no to others so that they are able to do something that they actually want to do. Fill this person with confidence without sounding like you are patronizing them. Tell them that their outfit looks great or that they have done a great job. Celebrate together too. Explore new places and even consider taking a class together so that you both empower yourselves with more knowledge. Laugh! Give your loved one a break from the nightmare they might be living and a chance to feel happiness.

Talk about situations in your life that require boundaries, such as how you feel when people cross them and what you do. This is far more productive than telling someone they need to set boundaries for themself when they have no idea where to start. You can do the same about moments when you need to assert yourself. Let them know that you were worried about how the other person would react but that in the end, the result was worth it.

Finally, challenge this person. Get them to ask for directions instead of you. Make them choose the film to watch or the next city to visit. This might seem like small challenges, but for them, it will be hard to make a decision based on what they want rather than what you want to hear. When your friend starts getting more confident in making choices, push them a little harder. For example, "No, I don't fancy that! What else have you got" and show great enthusiasm for the next idea. Teach them that it is okay that you don't always agree and that it is actually no big deal to have differing opinions.

Teaching Children and Young Adults to Be Assertive

Teaching young people how to assert themselves is a real gift for life. It can help them stand up to bullies and also to stand up for other people. They are able to feel more control over their lives, and this is when children can flourish.

One excellent method for younger children is the Stop, Walk, and Talk Method. When a child has issues with someone, whether it's a sibling or classmate, they will go straight to the adult. We want to teach them to first try to resolve the problem themselves:

- **Stop -** the child asks for the behavior to stop, and says, "Please don't take my toy."

- **Walk -** "I asked you not to take my toy," and then walk away.

- **Talk** - once they have asserted themself, then they go to an adult for help.

Understand the difference between a child talking and a child just trying to get the other person into trouble. Like with adults, children have to choose the battles that need to be fought. If another child is pulling faces, as an adult, you can't run in to save the day. Some things children have to learn to resolve by themselves so that they can become independent.

Be very clear about boundaries. It might be that your child isn't allowed fizzy drinks after dinner or homework is done without the TV on. Whatever boundaries you have set, it is crucial that you stick to them regardless of their age and the emotional tantrum they throw. Don't get angry with them for not being able to express how they are feeling correctly. Acknowledge their emotions and move on. But don't give in just for an easier life. It will teach children that boundaries hold no real weight.

Treat children how you like to be treated, whether they are your own children or your students. You want them to be kind, respectful, honest, and assertive, and therefore, you must treat them in the same way. There isn't one rule for you and another for them just because they are little. This isn't promoting the concept of equality.

Older children should be taught what assertiveness is and why it is so important in life. I know that it already feels like there isn't enough time in the day to teach what you need to, but taking one lesson or even half an hour to go over assertive behavior will save you a lot of time in the long run. You will find you can get through a whole class without someone inter-rupting you because of issues with behavior, insults, or snitch-ing. Role model assertive situation with examples of passive and aggressive behaviors. Going back to my university days, if only someone had taught me these essential life skills, I would have had a completely different life in my 20s and 30s than what I had.

In our final chapter, we are going to look at a plan when the need to assert yourself is too strong, and we can't wait for the process to naturally move from stage to stage. You may have some big decisions coming up or a large project that needs to be presented, and time is of the essence.

CHAPTER 16: ASSERTIVENESS TRAINING. YOUR STEP-BY-STEP ACTION PLAN FOR ASSERTING YOURSELF IN 21 DAYS

If you do feel like you are in a rush to assert yourself and you feel like you have taken on board all of the techniques we have worked through, you can start the 21-day assertive plan. Just remember, when you are at full-speed ahead, you will need to have a tougher shell. Be careful of rushing forward and letting unresolved feelings fester in case they end up having a knock-on effect.

At the same time, a 21-day plan is only an outline. I can't tell you to say no to someone on day four if the situation doesn't arise. While you were reading this book, you may have already begun putting some of the following steps into action, so that's great news, and you might be well on your way to asserting yourself.

Feel free to also change the order of the plan so that it feels more natural to you. Because we are all so individual, I'm not going to tell you how you should work through the action plan, only the order that worked for me. What is important is that each of the steps is covered.

So, here goes the 21 steps to change your life for the better, to get what you want and deserve without hurting those you care about.

Day 1. The Mentality

It's not about waking up and saying no. If your confidence is brimming, then, of course, you can start to assert yourself, but as you are enjoying your morning coffee or tea, let's think about our mentality.

Today is a new day. What has happened in the past has no reflection on your future. Mistakes were made, but we aren't going to dwell on them, rather we are going to learn from them.

I like to work on my fears first. Understand why you are scared to assert yourself. Is it the reactions of others or the fear of upsetting them? What makes standing up for yourself so hard?

You will be tempted to look back at times when people reacted negatively, but stop yourself. This is their reaction, not your feelings. List your fears in order from smallest to largest.

As we challenge ourselves in the next 21 days, we will start with the smaller ones and work our way up. Write them at the back of your journal. You don't want to open your journal each time and see your fears.

Keep telling yourself throughout the day that this is a fresh start. Make a mental note of anything that happens that you would like to handle differently.

Day 2. A letter to yourself

On the first page of your journal, I would like you to write a letter to yourself.

This letter is going to be telling yourself why being assertive is a good thing. It should include the improvement in communication and a strengthening of relationships.

You also need to tell yourself that you, like every other human being, deserve respect, love, and happiness; you have the right to live your life as you see fit.

Remind yourself that being assertive doesn't make you a bad person, and there is nothing to feel guilty about. That from today onward, you will make time to do the things you want, even if it means saying no to others.

Day 3. Learning about what makes you happy

If you have a choice between working overtime and sitting on the sofa contemplating life, it's easy to say yes to overtime. Let's dedicate a day to finding out what makes you happy.

What are your hobbies, your goals, your dreams? What things are you passionate about, or is there something new you have always wanted to try?

Make a list after the letter to yourself. When we have activities in our life that excite us, saying no is more appealing because there is something better to do than the option you are faced with.

Day 4. Affirmations and Visualization

Though both ideas may seem a little out there, they have been proven to make a huge difference in many people's lives. An affirmation is a short statement that is repeated in order to change your perspective and behavior. The repetition retrains your brain to respond in a positive way. Here are some suggestions:

• I am assertive

• I deserve to be happy

• My free time is my free time

• People respect my assertiveness

• I am responsible for only my feelings

When said with conviction, your brain will act in this way. Choose affirmations that ring true to you. Keep them in the present tense and always in positivity. Visualization is the same. Picturing yourself as a positive, confident person will allow you to feel this way. But, again, you have to believe your visual image and see yourself as you handle situations assertively.

Day 5. Observation day

Today, we are going to go about our day as usual but with extra attention to our feelings and emotions that arise in different situations.

How do you feel when the coffee pot is empty at work and you are always left to fill it? How do you feel when your mom calls you and asks you to come for family lunch when really you wanted to work in your garden?

If you feel prepared to assert yourself, you can, but don't put pressure on yourself. The most important thing is that you recognize your emotions.

Day 6. Exploring emotions

In our journals, we are going to write about the experiences and the emotions that are associated with each one. Then, using a thesaurus, we are going to look for related words that may express our feelings more clearly. Instead of saying angry, you could be "miffed" — slightly angry, or "furious." By finding a new vocabulary for different emotions, you will be better prepared to communicate with others.

Day 7. The practice run

You will have identified a certain behavior from a friend or relative that you would like to change. There is no need to go for the all-out 'no'; we are going to test the water, take one small step and overcome one or two of our smaller fears to build up our confidence.

Let's say your friend is a bit of a nag about your hair or your clothes. You would just have a short conversation to let them know. "I feel offended when you insult my clothes." See how this person reacts, look at their body language, and the certain signs we have learned about. Mirror their eye contact and posture.

This should be a person that you have great trust with. Once you have told them how you feel, you might want to tell them that you are learning to be more assertive and use this person for support and encouragement. Don't forget to celebrate this win—you are doing great!

Day 8. Start your new hobby

It sounds like an obvious one, but so often we brainstorm the things that we want to do but never get around to it. Without a new passion, you won't have alternative activities that you prefer to do. When you start thinking "I will do it next week, next month" you are delaying the process. If you haven't by now, sign up for that class or get on Amazon to buy the supplies that you need.

Day 9. Create a new challenge

New challenges are essential for building up our confidence. They allow us to explore our abilities and push our limits, giving us faith that we can achieve the things we want to.

Look over your list of fears and choose an activity that will enable you to overcome one. Remember, we are working our way up from the smallest.

For example, if you are scared of being alone in social situations, go to a restaurant alone. Prepare yourself, think of the worst thing that could happen, and then fill your mind with all of the positive things that will come out of it.

There will be nobody there telling you what to eat or drink, and you don't have to go to a restaurant that serves food you don't like.

Keep your challenge small and achievable.

Day 10. "I" statements

There are so many sentences that we have reviewed that will allow yourself to stand up for yourself in different situations. It is crucial you choose a few that you are confident using.

Some people are nervous about the simple "No, thanks" whereas those who get easily flustered prefer just two or three words. Choose a few for the times that you need to say no and a few for the situations where you need to express your feelings, for example, "I feel hurt when you ignore my opinions."

Day 11. Observation day 2

Now that you are more emotionally aware and you have your "I" statements prepared, it is time to watch others again, this time for body language.

When we start to assert ourselves, there is so much going on in our minds, and it is easy to forget a smile or having an open posture. By watching other people's body language and gestures, as well as the reaction of others, it will encourage you to be more aware of your own.

Day 12. Be assertive

It's time to take all of this and be assertive. Start your day with your affirmations, including "Today is going to be a good day." Do something to get the heart pumping and the blood flowing, even if it's just dancing to your favorite tunes. Shower and put on an outfit that makes you feel good about yourself.

No procrastinating here. If you keep putting it off, you may find that there are no more opportunities, and trust me, you will be disappointed. The excellent results from standing up for yourself early on in the day will encourage you to try again.

Day 13. Finding your stress outlet

Whether it is ongoing stress or the stress that arises from being assertive, it's necessary that you find a way to release this stress and let it out. Yoga, meditation, stress balls, relaxation games on your phone, a walk, a hot bath, a cold shower, etc. Each person will have that one thing that instantly calms them down. Find yours.

Day 14. Show off your new skills

The chances are this is going to sound very far out there, but even though you are still practicing, you have gained a substantial amount of information. Learning is amazing for confidence, but so is teaching.

While I am not suggesting you run a conference on assertive skills, today is a good day to tell someone else what you have learned so far. This will reinforce your learning, it will high-light what techniques have really stuck in your mind, and it will encourage you to revise others that you want to practice.

Above all, it will be great for your confidence, so talk to a friend or family member about what you have learned and put into practice.

Day 15. Setting your boundaries

Over the last two weeks, you will have learned a lot more about yourself, your emotions, and what you want from life. You should have a plan for how you want to get there. Knowing your boundaries will not only help you lead a happier life, but it will also help you to prevent setbacks that may occur from other people's behavior. It may mean looking back at situations in the past when people have crossed the line.

It's not a trip down memory lane to rehash the pain, just a lesson to understand what you are comfortable with and what you aren't. Use your journal to prepare when you would say when your boundaries are crossed.

Day 16. How does it feel to not be assertive

This might seem counterproductive, but you will be surprised by the results. By now, you will have gradually been building up your assertive moments, and things are probably going quite smoothly. There might have been some push back, but you have handled it well.

Today, you are not going to be assertive. This lesson will show you just how far you have come in such a short time. It will open your eyes to your progress and make you realize that you never want to go back to being a people pleaser. Day 1 changed our mentality. Today you can see the positive impact on your life, and you can be proud of the person you have become.

Day 17. Handling the manipulative person

After a day of not being assertive, you will be ready and determined to get back to the new you. You have learned to spot the person or people in your life that have been manipulating you, and now is the time to put a stop to it.

Don't feel you need to wait for the person to manipulate you again. Identify their behaviors and let them know how it makes you feel and that it has to stop. Be aware of further techniques they may use to manipulate you. Be very strong; don't fall for the tears or insults. "I am sorry you feel that way" and walk away.

Day 18. Reflection

It's time to look back over the last 17 days and see which techniques and statements you have felt comfortable using and perhaps look at some new ones that you might want to try.

It's also a good time to see how your emotions have changed over this time. Look at what areas of life you feel more confident in and others that you can work on. Decide if your new hobbies and activities are motivating you as you thought they would or whether you might like to change any of them.

Tick off those things you have achieved from your short-term goals to the fears you have overcome. Create your own action plan for the next following 21 days or month.

Day 19. Humor day

There are two reasons to dedicate a day to humor. First, laughing is such a great way to see the positive in the world and make you feel better about things.

Second, when it comes to introducing humor as a way to resolve conflicts, you will want to make sure you have an arsenal of tools. Check out some jokes or comic one-liner responses to different situations. Comedy series like *Friends* and *Frasier* have excellent witty comments that you can borrow.

Day 20. The Big One

If you have been working your way up knowing that there is a difficult situation or person that you have to deal with, today is the day. While knowing this might be the most difficult assertive moment so far, there is still no need to make it out to be more than what it is.

Remember cognitive distortion, you can't assume that the worst thing is going to happen when you don't have evidence to support it. At this point, you know what you need to do, and you will have your words carefully prepared. The most important thing is to make sure that your emotions are under control and that you have released the built-up tension in your body.

You have come so far, and you are so close to overcoming "the big one"—don't let them change your mind. Be firm, polite, positive, and, if necessary, tell them you will get back to them.

Day 21. It's all about you

This is your day to do whatever you want. An ideal goal to work toward over the 20 days is to say no to everything you don't want to do on this day. It should be completely free for you to enjoy in any way you want. There should be no obligations for you to dread on this day. Treat yourself. You have achieved a massive goal, and every goal needs a reward. Go out and get it. You have spent so long punishing yourself for the bad, it's high time you treat yourself for the good.

The 21-day plan should be completely flexible, and as I mentioned, it's not the right solution for everyone. You might need to spend two days on one step so that you feel more confident. If it takes you 30 days instead of 21, there is no shame, and you haven't failed in any way. If it takes you 10 instead of 21, that's great. It's not a race. It's a process that you should enjoy.

CONCLUSION

What a journey this has been. I know this will sound strange, but even though I haven't been physically present with you, I still feel proud of you. Looking back to some years ago, I can still see the person that I was: shy, nervous, often ill with stress. I was everyone's best friend but for all the wrong reasons. I didn't feel like I knew what my role was in any of my relationships. Knowing that you need to change and finding the strength to actually do it are two very different things.

We began this book as a caterpillar, and each step we took has helped us to transform into a butterfly—a little poetic, I know. Perhaps you feel more like an old banger of a car that has been restored to its original magnificence. The point is, there has been a change so significant, you can hardly recognize the new you.

The best part is that you have kept on to the kindness and good in your heart that you feared you would lose. Becoming an assertive person doesn't imply that you need to change your personality; it is about learning new skills so that you can improve as a person.

Choosing to read this book has allowed you to take all that is good about yourself and make it better. You will have built on your communication skills, which will have enabled you to not only learn more about yourself, but also more about those around you. By learning the importance of empathy, you can hopefully see people in a different light. Your nagging mom, who always wants to spend time with you, isn't trying to control your life. Instead, maybe she's just lonely. You can invest time in finding hobbies and activities for her so that you know she is happy, and you are able to live your life more independently. If a friend never does the things that you want to do and you are always stuck doing what they want, you have the knowledge and tools to explain how you feel and let them see things from your point of view.

Work stress is very much a real thing, affecting millions of lives each year. You have to be happy in your work since it's where we spend a huge portion of our day. The odd bad day at work is going to be normal, but when it's every day, we start to see the problems seeping into our evenings and weekends. Even when we aren't there, we are thinking about it. Setting boundaries for after work hours is the first step to taking back some control over your career. Being on call 24/7 doesn't make you the best worker, and nobody can maintain this lifestyle. Colleagues who take advantage of your kindness are only thinking of their own needs before yours, and this is not fair. The boss who can't control their temper or thinks it's amusing to humiliate you is crossing a boundary that they don't have the right to do. But this is okay, you now have the ability to stop this.

Learning the difference between passive and aggressive behavior will help you to keep your assertiveness in check, making sure you don't go from one extreme to the other, but whether you find the balance that is right for you. Don't worry if you make mistakes. A little too much eye contact will make the other person feel uncomfortable, but you will now be able to read their body language and learn from the next time. Don't be scared to say sorry if you feel that you have come across a little aggressive. We all make mistakes. What one person sees as aggressive might not be the same as the next, which is why every experience we have with assertion will allow us to learn more.

Keep up with your journal, even when you feel like you have mastered the art of standing up for yourself. It's an ideal way to monitor your emotions as times change. Life may throw a few curve balls at you, and you will appreciate having an outlet where you can comfortably work through how you are feeling.

At the same time, keep up with your goals, hopes, and dreams. Sometimes they will need adjusting, and other times you will reach your goals and will need to create new ones. Goals keep you motivated and focused and will help you to develop your confidence in a whole range of situations. Continue to explore new ways that will make you happy. There is a whole world out there, and we should take as much from it as we can. At the same time, don't forget to give back. Hold the door open for the old lady who pushed in front of you in the line, recycle, and remember that small acts of kindness are all opportunities to smile and be happy.

If I had to sum up this book in six simple sentences, this is what I would say:

• Learn more about who you are and what you want. Know that it is not only okay but good for your mental and physical health to put yourself first.

• Know your boundaries. Never let your values, beliefs, and opinions be disrespected or ignored. Respect other people's boundaries and ask questions before assuming you know how they feel.

• Don't feel you have to justify your answers. You don't have to explain yourself to anyone. You have the right to say no, full stop. Don't permit others to play on your feelings or manipulate you because they know you are a kind person.

• Keep your no's short, simple, and clear. Smile, make some eye contact, stand or sit up straight, be loud enough to be heard without shouting. If they are persistent, remind them that you have already said no.

• Take responsibility for your actions and your emotions. You cannot control what other people say or do. Their reactions are neither your responsibility nor your fault.

• Love yourself. Take time to relieve your stress. Look after and protect your body and your mind. Celebrate the good times, and don't punish yourself for the bad.

I hope you have enjoyed reading the book as much as I have writing it. I have given you the tools and techniques to go out and assert yourself, and I know deep down that you have the ability. If you like the book and it has helped you, I would love to hear your stories and opinions in a quick review on Amazon.

Keep feeling positive, know that you are going in the right direction, and congratulations!

SOME BOOKS YOU MAY FIND INTERESTING

Healthy Boundaries

How to Set Strong Boundaries, Say No Without Guilt, and Maintain Good Relationships With Your Parents, Family, and Friends

Discover the power of self-love, and learn how to set healthy boundaries – without feeling guilty.

Do you ever wonder what it would be like if the people you care about respected your personal space? Do you wish that there was an easy way to say "No" every time you don't want to say "Yes"?

If this is you, then you've probably had moments of trying to please others -- often, to your own detriment.

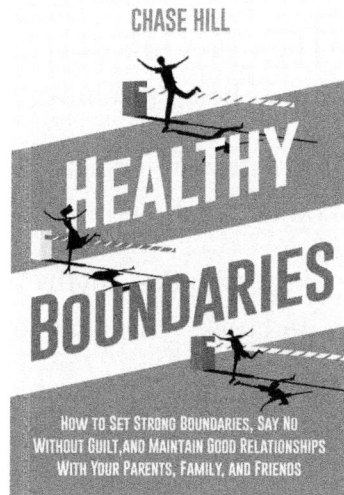

CHASE HILL

HEALTHY BOUNDARIES

HOW TO SET STRONG BOUNDARIES, SAY NO WITHOUT GUILT, AND MAINTAIN GOOD RELATIONSHIPS WITH YOUR PARENTS, FAMILY, AND FRIENDS

If this happens too often, eventually, people will start taking you for granted -- and you won't be taken seriously even when you try to say "No."

What's worse, when you do try to set up boundaries, people will label you as mean or moody. It will seem impossible to make people respect your decisions without starting conflict.

But there's a simple way to solve your problems!

You can start doing what YOU want to do. You don't have to compromise your individuality just to be "considerate" of others.

You can set healthy boundaries, and make your friends, family and parents **respect that boundary.**

In *Healthy Boundaries*, here's just a taste of what you'll discover:

• **A step-by-step guide to setting healthy personal boundaries without starting an argument**

• 5 dangerous mistakes you *must* avoid when setting boundaries

• The secret to saying "No" **without feeling guilty** -- and without being misunderstood

• How to stop constantly apologizing, and find out when you should and shouldn't be sorry

• 10 debilitating myths that are stopping you from setting up boundaries -- and how to troubleshoot them

• How to detoxify your emotions and release toxicity from your system like a breath of fresh air

• **A clear path** to give you the freedom to love yourself, follow what YOU want, and prioritize yourself

If you're ready to start living the life you deserve without feeling guilty, then scan this QR code right now!

SCAN ME

How to Stop Negative Thinking

The 7-Step Plan to Eliminate Negativity, Overcome Rumination, Cease Overthinking Spiral, and Change Your Toxic Thoughts to Healthy Self-Talk

There is a massive amount of shame that comes with negative thinking.

You blame yourself for the intrusive thoughts that blindside you. You feel guilty for not being more optimistic. **It's time to stop.**

Negative thinking isn't as simple as someone looking at the glass half empty. It is a **debilitating mindset** that seeps into every area of your life.

Negative thinking happens automatically – **it's not your fault.**

You tell yourself that today will be a better day, but your brain tells you the opposite, and you slip back into old negative habits.

But that doesn't mean that negative thinking is something you can't control.

The brain is indeed negatively biased. However, science has confirmed that **you can rewire the way you think**. And you can start doing this today!

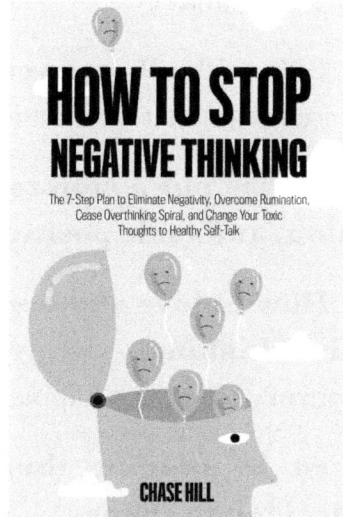

In *How to Stop Negative Thinking*, here is just a fraction of what you will discover:

• How to **overcome every type of negative thinking** from intrusive thoughts to rumination in 7 simple steps

• Simple, effective strategies with **practice exercises** that will help you overcome the negative thought patterns that prevent you from leading the life you want

• 3 crucial tools you can use to pinpoint the roots of your negative thinking

• **Scientifically proven breathing techniques** that will ease the impact of negative thoughts and rumination

• How to **put a stop to toxic behavior, passive aggression, and toxic positivity** and protect your new mindset

• **How to love and accept yourself despite your negative thinking** -- discover why this is crucial to kickstart your journey towards a happier, more positive person

Just by reading this, you have taken control and decided to change.

Now all that's missing is the final step.

If you are ready to take the next step towards a more positive life, then scan the QR code right now.

SCAN ME

Stop People Pleasing

How to Start Saying No, Set Healthy Boundaries, and Express Yourself

Do you say yes to people so often, you've forgotten how it feels to say no? You're not alone.

Many people spend years putting aside their own wants and needs in order to please the people in their life and avoid conflict. Although there will always be situations where diplomacy is important, **you cannot define your life through other people**.

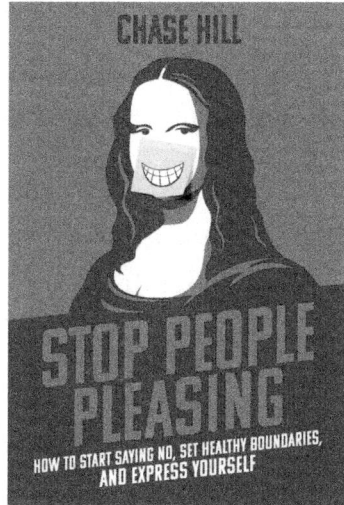

There's a fine line between being considerate of others, and compromising your individuality, and you can slip into living as a people-pleaser without even realizing it.

While these habits might seem to dominate everything you do, there are actionable steps you can take to create a new world-- one where you are open and confident in what you say and do.

Just like the relationships you have with others, everyone's experiences with people-pleasing are unique. However, this individuality often stems from common roots that are keeping you trapped in the box of others' expectations.

By helping you identify the steps that will assist you the most, Chase Hill shows it is possible to start changing, right here and right now.

In *Stop People Pleasing*, you will discover:

• The **10 signs** that indicate people-pleasing characteristics, besides the inability to say no

• A step-by-step **14-day action plan** to help you achieve instant and notable improvements

• The **4 defense mechanisms specific to people pleasing**, how to identify them, and how to respond to them

• Multiple exercises and approaches to help you rediscover who you are at heart, breaking free from feeling the need to seek validation from others

• Coping mechanisms designed to help you overcome discomfort or frustration as you redefine the boundaries in your life

If you believe it's impossible to finally stand up to your in-laws or be honest with your friends, think again.

You deserve to **make the choices that YOU want to make**, and speak your mind without fear or anxiety.

With the right tools and techniques by your side, you will be able to hit the ground running and be one step closer to living your life the way *you* want to live it.

If you're ready to finally stand up for yourself and transform your life, scan the QR code to order this book from Amazon page!

SCAN ME

How to Read People Like a Book

Speed-Read, Analyze, and Understand Anyone's Body Language, Emotions, and Thoughts

Stop racking your brain to figure out what others are really trying to say... know how to instantly decode the meaning behind their unspoken messages.

You don't have to be a communication expert, detective, or superhero to learn how to recognize and decode social cues. All you need to do is to know exactly what to look for and what they really mean.

Fortunately, this book contains everything you need to know about deciphering other people's silent messages.

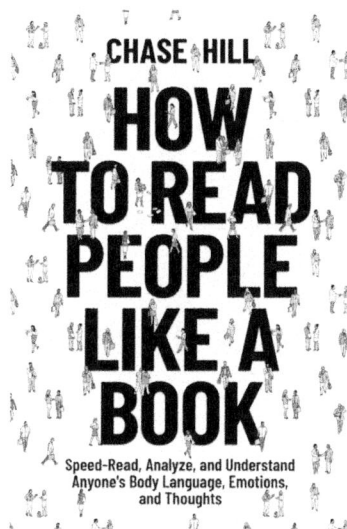

Inside, here is just a fraction of what you will discover:

• How to interpret facial expressions, body language, tone of voice, and other nonverbal cues – spare yourself from any miscommunication!

• **50+ social cues that will clue you in on what a person is thinking or feeling**... no more guessing games that could lead you to trouble

• What "clusters of gestures" are and why they are crucial to reading other people

- **25+ effective ways to tell if someone's lying – make any seasoned detective proud with your skills**

- Factors that affect how you read people – avoid getting the wrong conclusion about someone!

- **How to read between the lines using verbal cues... their choice of words matters more than you think!**

- Fool-proof ways to identify the tone of a text or email

And much more.

Every day, you encounter dozens of social cues without knowing how powerful they are or how you can use them to your advantage.

It's time to flip the narrative – by learning how to accurately read other people, you will not just boost your communication skills... you'll foster deeper connections and enjoy improved relationships more than ever.

Master the art of nonverbal communication and read people like a pro.

SCAN ME

A FREE GIFT TO OUR READERS

I'd like to give you a gift as a way of saying thanks for your purchase!

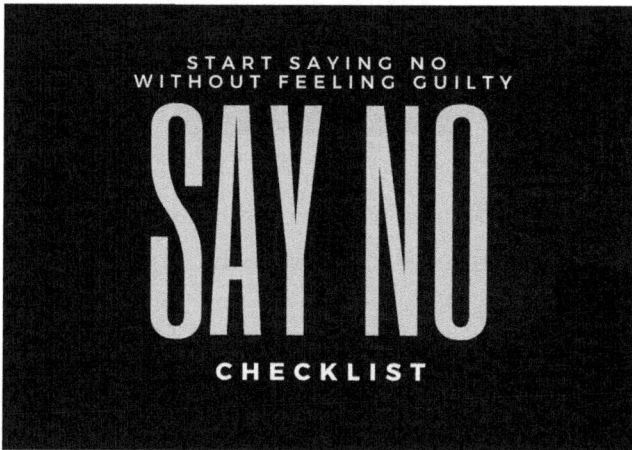

This checklist includes:

- 8 steps to start saying no.
- 12 must-dos to stop feeling guilty.
- 9 healthy ways to say no.

The last thing we want is for your mood to be ruined because you weren't prepared.

To receive your Say No Checklist, visit the link:

www.chasehillbooks.com

Prefer a quick access? Scan the QR code below:

If you have any difficulty downloading the checklist, contact me at **chase@chasehillbooks.com**, and I'll send you a copy as soon as possible.

REFERENCES

Ackerman, C. E. (2020, September 1). What is Self-Awareness and Why is It Important? [+5 Ways to Increase It]. Retrieved from https://positivepsychology.com/self-awareness-matters-how-you-can-be-more-self-aware/

Babauta, L. (n.d.). 25 Killer Actions to Boost Your Self-Confidence : zen habits. Retrieved from https://zenhabits.net/25-killer-actions-to-boost-your-self-confidence/

Baz Luhrmann - Everybody's Free (to Wear Sunscreen) Lyrics | MetroLyrics. (n.d.). Retrieved from https://www.metrolyrics.com/everybodys-free-to-wear-sunscreen-lyrics-baz-luhrmann.html

Bellis, R. (2016a, June 3). How Asserting Yourself (The Right Way) Can Also Help Your Team. Retrieved from https://www.fastcompany.com/3060427/how-asserting-your-self-can-also-help-your-team

Bellis, R. (2016b, June 3). How Asserting Yourself (The Right Way) Can Also Help Your Team. Retrieved from https://www.fastcompany.com/3060427/how-asserting-your-self-can-also-help-your-team

Brady, K. (2019, June 5). 5 Types Of Boundaries For Your Relationship. Retrieved from http://www.keirbradycounseling.com/types-of-boundaries-for-your-relationship/

Changing Minds. (n.d.). Assertive Body Language. Retrieved from http://changingminds.org/techniques/body/assertive_-body.htm

Conflict Resolution Skills - HelpGuide.org. (n.d.). Retrieved from https://www.helpguide.org/articles/relationships-communication/conflict-resolution-skills.htm

Egan, M. (2017, July 27). The Difference between Assertive and Aggressive. Retrieved from https://executivesecretary.-com/the-difference-between-assertive-and-aggressive/

Garey, J. (n.d.). How to Change Negative Thinking Patterns. Retrieved from https://childmind.org/article/how-to-change-negative-thinking-patterns/

How to Be More Confident: Increase Brain/Body-O2 Levels. (2019, November 14). Retrieved from https://www.normal-breathing.com/how-to-be-more-confident/

How To Get Rid Anger: 3 New Secrets From Neuroscience. (n.d.). Retrieved October 2, 2020, from https://www.bakadesuyo.com/2015/10/how-to-get-rid-of-anger/

Jennings, M. K. S. (2018, August 28). 16 Simple Ways to Relieve Stress and Anxiety. Retrieved from https://www.healthline.com/nutrition/16-ways-relieve-stress-anxiety#2.-Consider-supplements

Khalaf, O. (2018, June 15). Reactivation of recall-induced neurons contributes to remote fear memory attenuation. Retrieved from https://science.sciencemag.org/content/360/6394/1239

Lancer, D. (n.d.). 6 Keys of Assertive Communication - Family & Relationship Issues. Retrieved from https://www.grace-pointwellness.org/51-family-relationship-issues/article/56559-6-keys-of-assertive-communication

Marks, H. (2011, April 29). Stress Symptoms. Retrieved from https://www.webmd.com/balance/stress-management/stress-symptoms-effects_of-stress-on-the-body#2

Mayo Clinic. (2020, May 29). Being assertive: Reduce stress, communicate better. Retrieved from https://www.mayoclin-ic.org/healthy-lifestyle/stress-management/in-depth/as-sertive/art-20044644

NHS. (2020, July 20). Psychological therapies for stress, anxiety and depression. Retrieved from https://www.nhs.uk/condi-tions/cognitive-behavioural-therapy-cbt/

Platt, R. (2019, May 5). Teaching Assertiveness to Counter Meanness. Retrieved from https://www.middleweb.-com/40238/teaching-assertiveness-to-counter-meanness/

Robinson, L. (2019a, June). Managing Conflict with Humor - HelpGuide.org. Retrieved from https://www.helpguide.org/articles/relationships-communica-tion/managing-conflicts-with-humor.htm

Robinson, L. (2019b, September). Managing Conflict with Humor - HelpGuide.org. Retrieved from https://www.helpguide.org/articles/relationships-communication/managing-conflicts-with-humor.htm

Selig, M. (2012, October 1). Speak Up! 18 All-purpose Assertive Phrases. Retrieved from https://www.psychologytoday.com/us/blog/changepower/201210/speak-18-all-purpose-assertive-phrases

Smith, L. (2019, June 10). Yahoo is now a part of Verizon Media. Retrieved from https://uk.finance.yahoo.com/news/how-to-assert-yourself-at-work-when-you-have-anxiety-091831165.html

Steimle, J. (2016, January 12). 14 Ways To Conquer Fear. Retrieved from https://www.forbes.com/sites/joshsteimle/2016/01/04/14-ways-to-conquer-fear/

Tell The Difference Between Assertive, Passive and Aggressive Behaviour | | Counselling Service in FranceCounselling Service in France. (2012, September 11). Retrieved from https://counsellingservice.eu/tell-the-difference-between-assertive-passive-and-aggressive-behaviour

Whitmore, J. (2016, January 9). 7 Ways to Earn More Respect. Retrieved from https://www.entrepreneur.com/article/254761

Wikipedia contributors. (2020, September 30). Passive-aggressive behavior. Retrieved from https://en.wikipedia.org/wiki/Passive-aggressive_behavior

Printed in Great Britain
by Amazon